Physical Development in the Early Years Foundation Stage

This book aims to raise reader's awareness of how physical development impacts on all areas of learning and on general development. The author encourages practitioners to think about what physical activity actually means for children and the importance of balancing risk and challenge, then provides opportunities for children to be active and interactive and to use their senses to learn about the world around them.

Angela D. Nurse is an educational consultant.

Practical Guidance in the EYFS
Series Editor: Sandy Green

The *Practical Guidance in the EYFS* series will assist practitioners in the smooth and successful implementation of the Early Years Foundation Stage.

Each book gives clear and detailed explanations of each aspect of learning and development and encourages readers to consider each area within its broadest context to expand and develop their own knowledge and good practice.

Practical ideas and activities for all age groups are offered along with a wealth of expertise of how elements from the practice guidance can be implemented within all early years' settings. The books include suggestions for the innovative use of everyday resources, popular books and stories.

Titles in this series include:

Personal, Social and Emotional Development in the Early Years Foundation Stage
Sue Sheppy

Communication, Language and Literacy in the Early Years Foundation Stage
Helen Bradford

Knowledge and Understanding of the World in the Early Years Foundation Stage
Stella Louis

Creative Development in the Early Years Foundation Stage
Pamela May

Problem Solving, Reasoning and Numeracy in the Early Years Foundation Stage
Anita M. Hughes

Physical Development in the Early Years Foundation Stage
Angela D. Nurse

Planning for the Early Years Foundation Stage
Sandra Smidt

Physical Development in the Early Years Foundation Stage

Angela D. Nurse

Routledge
Taylor & Francis Group

LONDON AND NEW YORK

First published 2009
by Routledge
2 Park Square, Milton Park, Abingdon, Oxon OX14 4RN

Simultaneously published in the USA and Canada
by Routledge
270 Madison Avenue, New York, NY 10016

Routledge is an imprint of the Taylor & Francis Group, an informa business

© 2009 Angela D. Nurse

Typeset in Optima by
Taylor & Francis Books
Printed and bound in Great Britain by
TJ International Ltd, Padstow, Cornwall

British Library Cataloguing in Publication Data
A catalogue record for this book is available from the British Library

Library of Congress Cataloging in Publication Data
Nurse, Angela D.
  Physical development in the early years : foundation stage / Angela D. Nurse.
    p. cm. – (Practical guidance in the EYFS)
  Includes bibliographical references.
  1. Children–Growth. 2. Motor ability in children. 3. Child development.
  4. Human mechanics. I. Title.
  RJ131.N87 2009
  155.4'123–dc22   2008040853

ISBN 978-0-415-47906-6 (hbk)
ISBN 978-0-415-47905-9 (pbk)

Contents

Contents

Acknowledgements

In researching, writing and completing this book I have recognised my debt to all those children, including my own, who have puzzled, challenged and enthused me over the thirty-five years or so that I have been involved with very young children. In focusing here on physical development – always an aspect which I have considered neglected in comparison to other, discrete areas of development – I have realised how far the world has moved on in puzzling over and researching how young children learn to move and how this links to other aspects, particularly cognition. It has reinforced my long-felt belief that no element of child development can be separated fully from another. I thank the researchers who have given me such an interesting time in the weeks it took to write this. I need also to thank the generations of students who have taken my rantings on physical development, outside play and the nature of risk and challenge in our society to heart and have completed research and initiated projects that have improved the quality of so many little children's lives.

Finally, I need to thank the team that brought this book to fruition, especially Sandy Green. My greatest thanks, however, go to Phil, who not only acted as my research assistant, uncovering a great deal of up-to-date research information to support each chapter, but also as my mentor, sounding board and IT expert. It could not have been done without him.

Introduction

Aims

This book aims to provide support for practitioners who are responsible for the introduction of the Early Years Foundation Stage (EYFS). It focuses on the element of the Practice Guidance which refers to the physical development of children and intends to offer:

- a theoretical framework which examines accepted knowledge and explores new information from research; this is expected not only to consolidate practitioners' understanding of how children develop physically but also to ask them to consider the wider implications of neglecting this aspect of development and learning;

- ideas and activities for expanding on the new guidance and integrating these into every day practice and play.

The suggested activities are closely linked to the EYFS guidance so that learning outcomes can be observed, monitored and evaluated. They are accompanied by key questions which can be used in planning and implementing activities in this particular key area. The EYFS states as its requirement in this aspect of learning and development:

The physical development of babies and young people must be encouraged through the provision of opportunities for them to be active and to improve their skills of coordination, control, manipulation and movement. They must be supported in using

> all of their senses to learn about the world around them and to make connections between new information and what they already know. They must be supported in developing an understanding of the importance of physical activity and making healthy choices in relation to food.
>
> (DFES 2007b: 90)

Context

The current emphasis on early years is part of the UK Government's agenda to eradicate child poverty, to optimise development and to prevent early failure on entry to school in order to secure the UK's place in the global financial and political arena in the future.

As part of its strategy, the Government has introduced the EYFS to ensure that there is equality of opportunity for infants and children, who attend provision outside the home, from birth to six years of age. As the introduction to the EYFS states: 'All providers are required to use the EYFS to ensure that whatever setting parents choose, they can be confident that their child will receive a quality experience that supports their development and learning' (DCSF 2007: online).

To do this, the Government has:

- introduced a number of initiatives to improve the education and training of those who work closely with young children and their families;
- altered and augmented the inspection regime, combining education and childcare inspections;
- introduced curriculum guidance.

The EYFS is the most recent in the series. It brings together the *Curriculum Guidance for the Foundation Stage* (DfES 2000), the *Birth to Three Matters* (DfES 2002) framework and the *National Standards for Under 8s Daycare and Childminding* (DfES 2003). The Government's intention is clearly stated: this is 'building a coherent and flexible approach to care and learning' (http://www.standards.dfes.gov.uk/eyfs/site/about/index.htm). Underpinning this approach is *Every Child Matters* (DfES 2004), which defines these five outcomes for children:

1 be healthy;

2 stay safe;

3 enjoy and achieve;

4 make a positive contribution;

5 achieve economic well-being.

Since primary education in the UK became statutory nearly 140 years ago, there have been various reports into young children's health and development which offered good practice. In 1933, Sir William Hadow produced one centred on nursery and infant schools which contained 105 recommendations.

I thought that tunnel was long. ... I can do it! (3 years 5 months)

Practical and physical activities were paramount, set within an outdoors context. Health concerns and early identification of difficulties were highlighted as well as the need for good accommodation appropriate for such young children that would contrast with the poor housing in which many of them lived. The Hadow Committee's philosophy was encapsulated in these statements, which are totally relevant to the way in which the EYFS should be interpreted by practitioners today: 'Freedom and individual work are "essential" for the children', and 'freedom in planning and arranging her work is essential for the teacher if the ever present danger of a lapse into mechanical routine is to be avoided' (Gillard 2006: online).

The Plowden Report (1967) followed the thinking of Hadow. Then, in 1988, the introduction of the first version of the National Curriculum had serious implications for under-fives in most areas of the UK. This was at a time when child development had all but disappeared from initial teacher training for primary teachers, and nursery training was under threat. The beginning of the 1990s saw an influx of four-year-olds (and occasionally three-year-olds) into large infant classes, many totally unprepared for them and led solely by a teacher without other adult support. The curriculum had also moved to being far more formal. Limited play, long periods sitting, attending and listening and being prompted to undertake formal tasks, such as writing, for which they were not yet developmentally ready, became the fate of many young children. These factors may have increased the number of young children identified as having special educational needs. Physical development suffered perhaps most, although language skills (already causing concern twenty years or so ago) also appeared to weaken. These changes were sudden and dramatic.

The National Curriculum was not without its critics. Numerous reports and documents have now been published in response, which have championed the developmental needs of the youngest children, rather than conforming to the limited, formal educational, expectations implied by the National Curriculum. The final report of the Rumbold Committee (1990: Sections 54–5) for example concluded:

> The period from birth to age 5 is one of rapid growth and development, both physical and intellectual. At this stage, children's developmental needs are complex and interrelated.
>
> [...] Young children follow recognised patterns of development; but within any group of under fives there will be considerable variation between individuals. These differences are intensified because

very young children do not have in common the experiences provided by formal schooling. *Any attempt by educators to bring a common structure to their experience should take account of these variations, and should be designed to fulfil children's individual needs.*

(Rumbold 1990; italics in original)

During the same period, there were changes in the relationship between practitioners and parents. Paul (2008) highlights, admittedly from an American perspective, how many more parents now rely on expert advice, rather than instinct or familiarity with child-rearing. Not only do those who may have had a professional life of their own before coming to parenthood seek out experts, they also purchase books and educational toys, watch TV and DVDs and listen to radio broadcasts to learn how to become perfect parents. Other parents may be young and need support in different ways. The role of the practitioner, therefore, becomes not only to care for and educate the child but also to supply knowledge, support and comfort for those not at ease with parenthood. To do this, practitioners need skills with people, as well as knowledge, and to be secure in what they can find out in addition to what they know already. To be an expert professional in the field, the practitioner needs to acquire a thorough understanding of child development and of the impact of those closely involved with children as they start their journey through life.

Physical development in particular

This book considers physical development in infants and young children and how practitioners and others can support this in its fullest sense. It explores some theoretical aspects of physical development as well as presenting children's acquisition of skills in a time frame, though taking into account a *phase* approach to infant development, as well as a *stage* approach. Teachernet has provided an overview of child development to accompany the introduction of the EYFS and explains:

All children are different and to reflect this age ranges have been overlapped in the EYFS to create broad developmental phases. This emphasises that each child's progress is individual to them and that different children develop at different rates. A child does not suddenly move from one phase to another, and they do not make progress in all areas at the same time. However, there are some important 'steps' for each child to take along their own developmental pathway.

(Teachernet 2007: online)

It examines how physical development acts as a foundation for optimal development of other skills, such as language, and how good physical development is essential for healthy emotional development and well-being, as well as good general health. The links between what we know so far about the brain and how physical development is connected to, and integrated with, other skills and the senses will be explored. As well as supporting practitioners with fulfilling the specific expectations of the EYFS guidance, the book intends to offer an opportunity for practitioners to consider 'challenge' and 'risk' and what these mean in the context of young children growing and taking responsibility for themselves and their safety.

In many ways, physical development has been neglected in the past twenty years or so, losing out to an emphasis on more 'cognitive' aspects or 'academic' skills. Recently, however, there has been more stress on health and well-being through physical activity – with overriding concerns about childhood and later obesity – but the centrality of good physical development to other areas of human functioning does not seem to have been taken fully into account. Children's minds live in their bodies, so the two are inseparably interlinked. To ensure that all aspects of human performance and achievement are optimal, children need to develop control over their bodies, to integrate their skills and senses and then to understand and trust what they can do. They need to keep themselves healthy, both in mind and body, with a good sense of self-worth and achievement. The old saying 'healthy mind in healthy body' captures the fundamental importance of this. Hurst and Joseph, in their introduction to Doherty and Bailey's (2003: viii) publication, ask readers to 'rethink what we take so much for granted – the physical development and physical education of our young children'. Their argument is that because children are so naturally active from birth, 'We are sometimes inclined to forget just what a significant contribution physical competence and skill can make to the emotional and social well-being of children, as well as to their general health' (Hurst and Joseph 2003: viii).

Parker-Rees (2007: 14) underlines this in his statement that, 'Trying to understand how brains work without acknowledging their interaction with bodies is as futile as trying to understand how "individuals" function without acknowledging that they are situated in families and communities'.

This failure to appreciate how all areas of development are interlinked has led to an underestimation of the importance of the physical in educational legislation and documentation. Alongside the disproportionate emphasis on cognitive development, target-setting and limited training opportunities for those teaching young children, there has been a misunderstanding of how much of children's progress is determined not only by their genetic inheritance but also by the interplay with the environment in which they grow and with the older children and adults they meet who support development. Knowledge is essential to prevent practitioners, with all the good will in the world, attempting to teach developmentally inappropriate skills because the guidance and legislation lead us to believe that cognitive skills take precedence. Common sense tells us, for example, that teaching children to write their names, before they have practised and mastered fine hand-control movements, is a waste of time and can lead to poor self-esteem. It can be dangerous. Children may have problems later, if they develop a 'fist' grip early on when using a pencil or pen and are not then supported to refine this to an acceptable 'tripod' grip. Left-handers need special care to prevent a 'hook' grip developing (particularly in boys) which strains the wrist. A recent publication has explored 'hot-housing' where small babies are, for example, introduced to reading almost as soon as they are born; Paul (2008) has written about this parental acceleration of babies' development, posing the question that, if infants are led to concentrate on one aspect, such as language acquisition through signing, what other attributes are being neglected? She considers, 'A child who spends her days pursuing her own interests at a nearby playground or running through the aisles of the supermarket is acquiring the same developmental skills as the child ferried off to gym class twice a week for directed play, and far more cheaply' (Paul 2008).

 **EYFS**

The situation as it stood for young children at the beginning of the 1990s had to change. Increasing protests against the DLOs (Desirable learning outcomes on entering compulsory education, SCAA 1996) resulted in the Curriculum Guidance for the Foundation Stage (QCA 2000), closely followed by Birth to Three Matters (DfES 2002). A turning point in government thinking is apparent from the Post Report June 2000 from the House of Commons Education and Employment Select Committee into Early Years Education, which compared UK provision to models elsewhere and included reference to theory and relevant research, particularly in the development of the brain. This report owed a good deal to Christopher Ball's enquiry for the Royal Society for the Arts, *Start Right: the Importance of Early Learning* (Ball 1994).

Against this background, the EYFS must be seen as a move away from the political and economic towards recapturing the ground where child development and research go hand in hand. Nonetheless, there has been considerable criticism of the EYFS since its publication in September 2007. Most of this centres on its political intent, bringing in statutory guidance for children from birth onwards although statutory school age remains the term after a child becomes five years old. Critics see formality creeping in by the back door and fear, despite government reassurance, that inspectors will inspect to the detail of the EYFS rather than to its spirit. Strong practitioners should be able to support their philosophies and practices and collaborate with inspectors and others to make rational decisions and judgements.

There are those, of course, who consider that a more formal environment where children are *taught,* rather than supported to *learn* via a play-based curriculum, is preferable. Parents can still ask pointed questions about the value of play, but confident practitioners will be able to confirm this and support it from their knowledge. The role of the practitioner in early years provision can be seen as champion, friend and companion, enabler, observer, facilitator, mediator, role model, arbitrator and guardian and defender – as well as teacher. These descriptors have been gathered from all over the place and more could be added; essentially, each setting must decide what its philosophy is towards the role of adults as this crucially affects the way practice in the setting unfolds. Importantly, the early years practitioner also acts as an advocate for young children; in Mary-Jane Drummond's terms 'there are children in every community, ready and waiting for our best endeavours on their behalf' (Drummond n.d.).

This book intends to enable practitioners to reflect on the importance of good physical development as a firm foundation for other human developmental skills and to understand current theory and research which support this. By understanding what is required by the EYFS – and by taking it further – practitioners will also be able to reflect on the differences between 'risk' and 'challenge' in enabling young children to start to take responsibility for themselves from within a circle of safety. Practitioners will be able to justify their practice in terms of supporting young children, recognising the point each has reached and planning activities and opportunities for each to extend his or her skills and confidence in his or her own abilities. Practice in the UK can be contrasted with what happens elsewhere in the world, and the dilemma which is increasingly being debated over safety issues compared with essential opportunities for optimal physical growth and development will be explored later.

Practitioners should keep in mind the words of Carla Rinaldi, who leads the Reggio Emilia programme and who stated in an interview with Lella Gandini, 'The potential of a child is stunted when the endpoint of their learning is formulated in advance' (quoted in Edwards et al. 1998: 118).

Reading and resources

Each chapter contains direct reference to the EYFS, though I have taken the liberty of selecting the most appropriate for each chapter and sometimes changing the order in which they appear in the full documentation.

The sources used to inform this book are varied and should give a wide enough sample for those who are already interested and knowledgeable about physical development and who wish to expand their understanding to follow this through to the more detailed publications and research reports. For others who are relatively new to this at a deeper level, there are texts which are more easily accessed. For those who share concerns about risk and challenge, there are a number of sources they can access, particularly verified websites. For readers who are captivated by the history and context of early years care and education and want to consult original documentation, David Gillard's website (www.dg.dial.pipex.com) provides access to an ever increasing collection of relevant reports and legislation which are difficult to unearth elsewhere.

All the examples included in each chapter are 'real life', taken from my experiences over a long period as a teacher, adviser (often working with parents in their own homes) and lecturer. In consideration of ethical issues, these have been adjusted and details altered so that the original sources cannot be identified. There are also examples which are based on my experiences as an elder sister with two younger brothers, as a mother and now as a grandmother. The majority of photographs are of my brood and they have been used with their permission.

In revisiting this aspect of child development, there is no intention at all to undermine the existing knowledge held by the majority of practitioners who work with very young children. It must be said, however, that the rapid expansion in childcare and education over the past ten years or so has left many new practitioners, whether already professionally qualified or new to the field, with a lack of confidence and sense of inadequacy when it comes to an in-depth knowledge of how very young infants and children grow and learn. This is particularly so for teachers who will probably have had little in their initial training that refers to three- to five-year-olds' development, let alone the development of those younger than three, unless they hold a specialist degree in early childhood studies or psychology, for example, or have taken an advanced early years programme in their initial teacher training. Hopefully this will be rectified soon with the introduction of the graduate Early Years Professional Status (EYPS), which, the Children's Workforce Development Council claims, 'has been introduced in response to this evidence to develop high quality services that will support the wellbeing, learning and development of all children' (www.cwdcouncil.org.uk).

For those practitioners who already hold knowledge of child development and practical experience of children from birth to six years of age, the book hopes to offer an opportunity for reflection on the current state of knowledge and research findings. Knowledge is not static, and, rather than just providing activities that match the expectations of the EYFS, a thorough understanding of what is involved in supporting a child's optimal development will enable practitioners to devise their own activities from a basis of deeper understanding, interest and curiosity. This book aims not to be just a 'how to' book but always to also pose the question 'why?'

To simplify discussion and referencing within the text, I have termed all publications emanating from government sources as 'government publications', whichever political party has been in power. This is also because ministries have been reorganised and renamed so many times in the past two decades that it is hard to recall where we are now. Exact details, however, can be obtained from the references at the end of each chapter. Finally, I have also generally used the term 'practitioner' throughout the book unless there is a need to highlight a particular professional background. This reflects the myriad of qualifications and professional heritages rampant in the early years sector. It is purely used as a shorthand catchall, never intended to disregard the importance to the individual of the professional pathway he or she has chosen and never in disrespect.

Example 1: happy families

Tina sits at home with her new baby. Just a few days old, the baby has already established feeding and is content. Tina is pleased she seems to have avoided the 'baby blues' and is getting to know her new child. She gently rocks her and notices when the baby copies her own facial expressions and she copies hers. Her elder daughter, just three, is already involved with her new sister. She loves to run errands for her mum, particularly running upstairs to fetch things. She has recently become far more confident at climbing stairs on her own. She likes to practise without holding on and can walk up them now like mummy, alternating her feet on to each stair. She sits next to mum on the settee and threads a necklace for baby; because the baby is small, she chooses the smallest beads...Tina is already working out how to present the gift to the baby without hurting her elder daughter's feelings and harming the baby! Tina strokes her elder daughter's hair, enjoying this moment together. The TV, for once, is off and Tina takes the opportunity to narrate the stories of her childhood to her daughters, telling of climbing and running in the woods with her brothers and sisters and her friends. They had built camps and played games in the trees with a freedom she would love to offer her children, but they live in the inner city. Outside, her son, now five and a half, pedals his bike on their small patio. He has just learnt to ride his bike without stabilisers and is very proud of himself. He has created an obstacle course with chairs and boxes and is learning to ride around them. He is able to work the lights and sound the bell on his bike while doing this. He has just returned from swimming with his dad and is doing well. He is not frightened of the water and is beginning to swim, though he is not yet ready to remove his armbands. Tina recognises how much energy he has at this age and tries to provide him with activities to use it up and the freedom to challenge himself in the garden. He often plays with a neighbour who is a year or so older, and this provides him with a model. Tina sometimes winces at the antics they get up to, but then remembers her own childhood and how she learnt to cooperate, to test herself and to follow instructions with her peers. She recovered from numerous bumps and bruises and so will he. Tina is seeing the effects of this in school. Her son attends a newly reorganised EYFS unit and he is settling well. The practitioners understand and share Tina's philosophy and feed back to her that, although he loves to be outside, her son will settle and attend to storytime and is interested in small-world and construction materials. He often revisits what he has been doing in his play with these materials, relating and expanding on the events he has experienced. One of the staff will write his stories down, and he is interested in adding photos or drawings. He is proud of the book he is creating and brings it home to share with his parents.

Questions

Reflect on your initial training and consequent professional development:

- How much of this was dedicated to an understanding of child development, particularly the physical and sensory aspects?

- Has this prepared you fully for the complexities of your current role? Share this with your colleagues.

- What do you know and what do you need to find out now about young children's physical development? On what will you base your knowledge?

- Why is good self-esteem so important? What makes you feel good about yourself? How can we ensure that children feel good about themselves? Why is this an important factor for mental health?

- Consider the knowledge and skills you need to have as an early years practitioner. What are the essential qualities you need to demonstrate in working with parents and their children?

As a starting point, consider Example 1 above. Referring to the EYFS Practice Guidance (2008), how would you respond to these discussion points?

- Look, listen and note;

- Effective practice;

- Planning and resourcing.

References

Ball, C. (1994) *Start Right: The Importance of Early Learning,* London: Royal Society for the Encouragement of Arts, Manufactures & Commerce.

Department for Children, Schools and Families (DCSF) (2007) 'The Early Years Foundation Stage'. Available online at http://www.standards.dfes.gov.uk/eyfs.

Department for Education and Employment (DfEE) (2000) *Curriculum Guidance for the Foundation Stage* (0500/QCA/00/587), London: DfEE.

Department for Education and Skills (DfES) (1988) *Education Reform Act*, London: HMSO (introduced The National Curriculum).

Department for Education and Skills (DfES) (2002) *Birth to Three Matters,* London: DfES, Sure Start Unit.

—— (2003) *Full Day Care: National Standards for Under 8s Day Care and Childminding,* Nottingham: DfES.

—— (2004) *Every Child Matters: Change for Children,* Nottingham: DfES.

—— (2007) *Practice Guidance for the Early Years Foundation Stage,* London: DfES.

Drummond M.-J. (n.d.) *The Report: 5x5x5 in Context: Challenges and Changes,* London: National Endowment for Science, Technology and the Arts. Available online at http://www.5x5x5creativity.org.uk/cms/user_files/files/Nesta555Report.pdf.

Edwards, C., Gandini, L. and Forman, G. (1998) *The Hundred Languages of Children: The Reggio Emilia Approach – Advanced Reflections,* 2nd edn, Greenwich, Conn.: Ablex.

Gillard, D. (n.d.) 'Education in England'. Available online at http://www.dg.dial.pipex.com (accessed 21 May 2008).

The Hadow Report (1933) *Infants and Nursery Schools*, London: Board of Education.

Hurst, V. and Joseph, J. (2003) 'Series Editors' Preface', in J. Doherty and R. Bailey, *Supporting Physical Development and Physical Education in the Early Years,* Buckingham: Open University Press.

Paul, P. (2008) *Parenting Inc.* New York: Times Books.

The Plowden Report (1967) *Children and their Primary Schools*, London: DES.

Rumbold Report (1990) *Starting with Quality*, London: HMSO.

School Curriculum and Assessment Authority (SCAA) (1996) *Desirable outcomes for children's learning on entering compulsory education,* London: HMSO.

Select Committee on Education and Employment (SCEE) (2000) Post Report 140, June. Available online at http://www.teachernet.gov.uk/teachingandlearning/eyfs/childdevelopment (accessed 21 May 2008).

Willan, J., Parker-Rees, R. and Savage, J. (eds) (2007) *Early Childhood Studies,* 2nd edn, Exeter: Learning Matters.

1

Theoretical perspectives

What we currently know about how the body works

Aims

At the end of this chapter you will have recognised the two strands of research that apply to your work as an early years practitioner. First, you will have started to become familiar with 'scientific' research that has taken place in the past and is currently being undertaken in the field of physical development, health and well-being in the very young. Second, you will begin to recognise how the term 'research' applies to enquiries that you may undertake in your setting to, for example, gauge the effectiveness of changed routines or the introduction of new forms of experience. A brief discussion on research methodology and the importance of critically understanding the context and process of research will enable you to start to analyse the outcomes of this research and their relevance to your provision.

Introduction

It has often been argued in the UK that teaching and research proceed in parallel but rarely meet to inform each other. It appears that the rift has been more to do with distrust, even dislike, with overtones of an 'ivory tower' syndrome. It is usually difficult to discern where the relevant results of research (the other 'three Rs') have impacted fully on educational practice. Over the past twenty years, the Government's attitude towards young children's education and care has begun to alter, and this marrying together

I climbed up the tree – so did the ant (2 years 9 months)

of research and practice has become more evident in reports and guidance. Now, the Sure Start website provides direct links to important research reports that impact on early years provision.

There has been recognition that the care and education of the youngest children is complex and involves understanding a great deal from a number of disciplines. To offer those who were interested and to provide progression routes for practitioners in the field, well over a decade ago universities started to develop degrees in early childhood studies which include a strong emphasis on research – both what researchers are finding out and the place of personal research in the workplace. This has been continued through the development of specific foundation degrees and now the EYPS. Many early years graduates are now moving on to programmes at masters level and beyond. At the same time, programmes have been on offer in initial teacher training, such as the postgraduate certificate in education (PGCE) in advanced early years, which have emphasised these aspects within their preparation for teaching.

The impact of research

How much of this change has been the result of research into childhood in recent years? Some of it undoubtedly has, particularly in infant brain development; for example, the Government published *Post Report 140* following a House of Commons Education and Employment Select Committee enquiry into early years education. The report intended to offer a resumé of research as follows:

> First, research on the development of the brain and its relevance to early years education […] Next, research on the development of sensory, cognitive and emotional skills in children [with] possible implications for early years education […] [Finally] studies that have compared the outcomes of different types of pre-school education […] to assess the type of early years experiences that best suit the developing child's needs.
>
> (SCEE 2000: 1)

This interesting enquiry was set in the context of many UK children, especially in England, attending formal infant classes at four years of age. It drew on named research studies from not only the UK but also the USA and Europe, summarising: 'Research suggests that children under the age of four or five may not have fully developed the social and cognitive skills that facilitate learning from formal instruction' (SCEE 2000: 12). More pertinently for the purposes of this book, it concluded, 'Such research has led some to question the value of formal education at an early age and to suggest that *a focus on social interaction, play and exploration might be more valuable*' (SCEE 2000: 12; my italics).

This was published at a time when the original curriculum guidance (*Desirable outcomes for children's learning on entering compulsory education* [SCAA 1996/DLOs]) was being revisited in response to practitioners' anxieties, parental concerns and media campaigns which looked at systems in other countries in contrast to the UK. This original document, put together very quickly, owed little to knowledge let alone 'practical' or 'scientific' research. Within the UK, Wales was beginning to move away from what it saw as a too formal and rigid early years system to develop one of its own which owed far more to child development and research. Scotland published its own guidance which included a booklet on Reggio Emilia, revised in 2006 (Scottish Consultative Council on the Curriculum 2006).

Physical development in particular

Research that supports the physical development strand, in its widest interpretation, can be divided into:

- brain development;
- motor development;
- health;
- well-being.

Overwhelmingly, the whole area of neuroscience has dominated the early years sector in the past few years. In many ways this has been welcome, because it has given scientific, therefore acceptable, proof to what early years practitioners have always known about how children develop and what they need to do this successfully. David et al. (2003: 118) reviewed what is known about young brains, reflecting:

> There are conflicting views about the extent to which environmental influences and stimulation shape early brain development and subsequently impact upon one's later physical and mental well-being. There are opposing views whether missed (or neglected) opportunities during early brain development can be regained later in life.

The brain has been described as the last unexplored territory on Earth, but many neuroscientists would say that the more we find out, the less we seem to know for certain. Although we possess the ability to see and measure what happens when the brain is stimulated through various brain imaging techniques, the apparatus that does this is still fairly crude. Minute details of what is happening cannot yet be isolated, though we now know that babies are born with many more neurons than they will need but need to make connections between these neurons to ensure their capacity to control the body, learn and understand. The role of experience, therefore, is crucial in making these connections, and there are 'sensitive' periods when it is easier for the brain to do this. The brain, however, is flexible and the connections can be made later, but perhaps not without more effort. Some findings from this research may seem contradictory and in need of interpretation, but it seems sensible to suggest that there is now agreement that the earliest years of a child's life are instrumental to optimal development in the later years.

As the UK begins to focus much more on physical development, results from other enquiries and research reports are being published. Recently these have included a review by the National Institute for Health and Clinical Excellence (NICE) presented in May 2008 and research into play and exercise by the National Children's Bureau (NCB), commissioned by the Department for Culture, Media and Sport (April 2008). Both of these stressed the value of outdoor play and the importance and of quality in the resources provided, in design and in sensitive adult support. The latter stressed the importance of 'ethos' in good provision. Both provide substantial lists of sources for further reading; the NCB report is structured as a research report for those who are interested in pursuing research further.

What does 'research' mean?

'Research' carries a number of different meanings and it is important to distinguish between them and understand the varied methodologies if its value is not to be dismissed out of hand. Particularly during the 1920s and 1930s, research into children's development moved towards becoming, in the eyes of those involved, more 'scientific'. The early observations of individual children, termed 'baby biographies', led to generalisations about developmental norms in a whole population, and the emphasis on 'experimental design' was intended to counter this and make researchers' results more acceptable academically. Ethical standards were far different in these early days and some of the experimentation would be considered abusive today. Different conceptions of society and the child are explored by Prochner and Doyon (1997) who suggest 'a lack of sentimentality in relation to subjects was the hallmark of the scientist of the period'. Researchers then often wished to remove children from their natural environments, including their families, so that outcomes were not tainted by variables beyond their control. Techniques are far more sophisticated today and are covered by strict ethical considerations, but there is still this concern that children are often observed in the laboratory rather than in their own environments, though this is not always so. This belief has coloured many practitioners' visions of the worth of scientific research and how valuable it is in the practical life of the early years setting. We need to move beyond that to considering what has been discovered that will aid our understanding of the individual or the group.

There are a number of books now that support practitioners through the research process, with an emphasis on working with children and the ethical considerations which must be taken into account when any form of research is undertaken. In helping practitioners to understand research, there are a number of aspects that practitioners must consider. This includes crucial information about who initiated the project and (if applicable) who paid for it, how it was designed and the methods used.

What was the research question? Was it clear? Details of sample size, how it was selected and whether it truly represents the population it was researching are important points. Was it a *longitudinal* study (i.e. following up the same set of subjects over a period of time), or was it *cross-sectional*, a snapshot of a sample at one particular time? If it included interviews, did the questions lead the participants to answer in a particular way or were they totally open-ended? How were the results analysed, and did outcomes honestly lead from the gathered information? Was the original question answered? Practitioners should consult original sources and not just heed 'sound bites', so often presented by the media which fail to report the whole picture, because that is not their job. For those who read newspapers (or who mark student assignments!), it is always galling to read 'research has shown...' when no reference is made to who has done it, how it was done and what the full conclusions were, rather than selected fragments which only support the point being made.

There are many research studies which are of interest to the early years practitioner. Some are longitudinal, such as High/Scope, the 1958 National Child Development Study and the 1970 British Cohort study, all now followed up over a number of decades. Details of these can be found at the Centre for Longitudinal Studies at the London Institute for Education's website, along with the more recent Millennium Cohort study. Scotland has inaugurated its own longitudinal study, *Growing Up in Scotland*. Starting in 2005, it is following 8,000 children and has just reported its second sweep. Part of this is designed to look at children's health in detail.

Child development

Changing perspectives on child development were highlighted in the Introduction, and this section expands on the points made there. Research is now under way, but there was a period from the first half of the twentieth century through to its later decades, where the work of scientists led to the conclusion that physical development followed a generalised pattern, due to maturation, that was rarely bypassed. This mainly followed Gesell's (1880–1961) work: stages and milestones were set and have formed the basis for judging progress until recently. Adolph et al. (2003) concluded because of this that 'from the 1950s to the 1980s, motor development was virtually ignored by developmental psychologists.' Piek (2006: 34) summarises the theories of *maturationists* such as Gesell and his colleagues: 'The morphogenesis of human behaviour, therefore, is subject to lawful sequences which normally are never circumvented'.

Piek points out that much of this theory rests on the fact that the researchers were looking for 'norms' and disregarded anything that was beyond these that 'may be an indicator of abnormal development' (2006: 39). It is now recognised that this is not so and this simplistic approach to motor skills is being revisited. Children can, and do, miss out 'stages' in their physical development and still get to the same point as others at roughly the same time. One of the numerous criticisms voiced against this way of viewing how children develop is that it ignores context and culture and is predominantly based on advantaged white children of European descent. Adolph et al. (in press) illustrate this neatly: 'Researchers have gathered little data about the effects of extreme climates and physical conditions on motor development, and little is known about the acquisition of motor skills that seem rarified in our culture (climbing, swimming, pounding, using dangerous implements) but are commonplace in others'.

The World Health Organisation's (WHO) Multicentre Growth Reference Group (2006) collected data from six diverse countries in a longitudinal study that revisited the times by which milestones were reached in healthy children. Instead, they developed 'windows of achievement' to reflect the time frames by which individual progress could be checked (see Appendix 1). Sitting without support, for example, is considered to appear between 3.8 months and 9.2 months, with an average of 6 months. What the researchers admit they did not know was, if the infant had not yet achieved sitting or walking, when this was likely to happen: it could be tomorrow or in three months' time. At the time of testing, any two children could appear identical. They emphasise: 'for any two children who exhibit the milestone on the day of the survey, we would be unable to differentiate between them with regard to development because we do not know when they performed the milestone for the first time' (Multicentre Growth Reference Group 2006: 94).

This is interesting and pertinent to practitioners' work with infants and parents. It reveals a much more sensitive approach towards development and cautions care in comparing one infant with another. Most children get where they want to go eventually but take different pathways.

Personal research

This chapter ends with a plug for more research in the early years. Practitioners, teachers in particular, are now encouraged to undertake small-scale research in their settings. The National Teacher Research Panel sponsors researchers, and the results are published at a conference and online. The Children's Workforce Development Council (CWDC) also publishes practitioner-led research: 'PLR [Practitioner-led research] is a programme which provides funding for practitioners to carry out their own small-scale research project into their area of work. Each practitioner designs their own research and sets their own research question and no previous experience of research has been required' (http://www.cwdcouncil.org.uk/plr).

These sponsored projects are published on the CWDC website. An example from the 2006–7 set is Michelle Shewring's investigation into children's reactions to mixed-age childcare settings, whose findings include how much children learn from older children, how they would ask for help from them rather than an adult and how play in mixed age groups is more often child-led. Interestingly, however, she also recognised that children needed time to play with others of a similar developmental level as 'children can find constant exposure to children of a different developmental level quite stressful' (http://www.cwdcouncil.org.uk/plr-projects-2006–07).

Practitioner research can offer opportunities to develop observational skills and to explore an area of interest, to investigate an issue or to try to solve a problem. For the unsure, there are always people with more experience to advise and help, so that the design of the research and the way in which the data are collected and then analysed answer the question defined at the beginning.

Example 2: Beyond the book

Sally was always forward in her physical skills, according to the book. As a new mother with next to no experience of small babies, this was her mum's bible until she learnt to trust her own judgement and threw it aside. Sally always managed to beat the book by a month or two, even outwitting her grandmother. At just 5 months she was rolling from front to back, then managed to roll from back to front a couple of weeks later. Unfortunately she was on the bed at the time but survived the fall (Sheridan (2008) estimates that rolling from back to front usually occurs between 6 and 7 months). Having accomplished this, two weeks later she was determined to crawl. Her first attempts to reach a toy resulted in her creeping backwards – and a display of frustration and temper – but less than a fortnight later she had mastered the art of the forward crawl. At 6 months, then, she had her world at her fingertips, though she neglected to establish the gentle art of sitting up unaided before she was off. At this point, her mum had to return to work, and Sally was looked after by her grandmother. Nan found her on several occasions sitting at the bottom of the stairs, crying. Sally lived in a flat at the time, and she did not have access to stairs there. Wanting to solve this puzzle, next time the door was open and she headed in that direction, her mum quietly followed. To her amazement, Sally hauled herself up the full flight of stairs. (Sheridan (2008) offers 12 months as the earliest point that infants *may* attempt stairs.) Unsurprisingly, Sally was walking confidently at 11 months. By 12 months, she had also mastered the neat trick of climbing a ladder to follow her father into the attic. One other antic comes clearly back to mind because it amazed her parents. Sally had woken very early one morning, and, in need of more sleep, her parents had taken her from her cot and had put her on the floor to crawl around. She was 6 months old and had not been crawling for long. She crawled on her hands and knees and could steer around obstacles. Of course her mum did not return to sleep but dozed fitfully with one eye on her. Her cot side was down, leaving a gap of perhaps 20 centimetres or so. Sally managed to crawl under her cot and was heading for an escape where the cot side was down. Her parents waited for the crunch and then tears. They did not come. Sally, without hesitation, lowered her head to the floor, flattened her body and crawled straight under.

Her mum was fascinated by Sally's physical prowess. Was it something inherited? Her mother could remember no details of her earliest days, apart from potty training. She could remember one of her younger brothers being particularly active but not the details, rather a sense that he, too, did things before he was expected to. Sally's father was apparently a 'bottom-shuffler' and did not walk till quite late. Her sister, born a month prematurely, took her first independent steps at 10 months but so surprised herself that she sat right down, and it was another month before she gathered herself together and took off confidently. Sally's son was also walking at 11 months. Yet other skills, such as potty training and talking, were at the other end of the scale for each. All, however, despite the precocity in developing physical skills and lateness in acquiring others, were not 'out of the ordinary' in later childhood or as adults.

Example 3: Freedom to move

Vicky is five and has cerebral palsy that affects her mobility, fine motor skills and speech. She attends the early years unit in her local school, which is flexible in meeting children's developmental rather than chronological needs. With her parents' agreement, she has been able to extend the period in which she spent much of her school day in physical activity. She crawls and rides a trike though she cannot yet walk. She becomes very tired through this, and space has been found for her to rest after lunch. She has someone to support her, but she likes to be independent and it is not thought good practice for her to become over-dependent on one-to-one help. She is learning to communicate her wishes via the computer, but her parents have been advised that learning to write eventually will help her fine motor skills, her sense of achievement and her memory for motor patterns through those needed for writing. They are encouraged to let her practise lots of large motor movements in drawing and painting. The school invested in the Write Dance programme to help her and other children needing some support. Surprisingly for the staff, her parents and the advisory support team, Vicky learns to colour beautifully and gains great satisfaction from doing this. During one advisory visit, the teacher is discussing her progress with a member of staff (in front of her!). Vicky listens to what they have to say about her – learning to use large movements in her writing before moving on to writing in a conventional size – and decides to prove everyone wrong. She carefully writes her name in small script in the top left-hand corner of her colouring, then looks up and grins.

Questions

- What two aspects of research are relevant to your role as an early years practitioner?

- Have you already used any research strategies to solve a problem within your setting or to clarify an issue to do with children's learning? What were these and how did what you found out add to your understanding and practice?

- What piece of research has had most impact on you and your practice?

- How can you ensure that the research results you use come from a reliable source and are applicable to your setting?

- How can you ensure that research findings are disseminated within your setting and to your parents and that relevant findings have an impact on your provision?

As a starting point, consider the Examples above. Referring to the EYFS Practice Guidance (2008), how would you respond to these discussion points?

- effective practice;

- look, listen and note;

- planning and resourcing.

References

Adolph, K. E., Weise, I., and Marin, L. (2003) 'Motor Development', in L. Nadel (ed.), *Encyclopedia of Cognitive Science,* London: Nature Publishing Group, pp. 134–7.

Adolph, K. E., Karasik, L. B. and Tamis-LeMonda, C. S. (in press) 'Moving Between Culture: Cross-Cultural Research on Motor Development', in M. Bornstein (ed.) *Handbook of Cross-Cultural Developmental Science,* Vol. I: *Domains of Development Across Cultures,* Englewood Cliffs, NJ: Lawrence Erlbaum Associates.

Brady, L.-M., Gibb, J., Henshall, A. and Lewis, J. (2008) *Play and Exercise in the Early Years: Physically Active Play in Early Childhood Provision,* London: NCB and Department for Culture, Media and Sport.

David, T., Goouch, K., Powell, S. and Abbott, L. (2003) 'Young Brains', in *DfES Research Report Number 444: Birth to Three Matters: A Review of the Literature,* Nottingham: DfES.

Gesell, A. and Thompson, H. (1934) *Infant behaviour: Its genesis and growth,* New York: McGraw-Hill

NICE (2008) Physical Activity and children: Review 8. Review of Learning from Practice: Children and Active Play. Final Draft, London: NICE/NHS.

Piek, J. (2006) *Infant Motor Development,* Champaign, Ill.: Human Kinetics.

Prochner, L. and Doyon, P. (1997) 'Researchers and Their Subjects in the History of Child Study: William Blatz and the Dionne Quintuplets,' *Canadian Psychology/Psychologie Canadienne,* 38 (2): 103–11.

SCAA (1996) *Desirable outcomes for children's learning on entering compulsory education,* London: HMSO.

SCEE (2000) Post Report 140, June. Available online at http://www.teachernet.gov.uk/teachingandlearning/eyfs/childdevelopment (accessed 21 May 2008).

Scottish Consultative Council on the Curriculum (2006) *The Reggio Emilia Approach to Early Years Education,* Glasgow, Learning and Teaching Scotland.

Shewring, M. (2007) *Children as Partners in a Holistic, Naturally Grouped Environment,* Leeds, CWDC.

World Health Organization (WHO) Multicentre Growth Reference Study Group (2006) 'Windows of Achievement for Six Gross Motor Development Milestones', *Acta Paediatrica,* Supplement 450: 86–95.

2 | What physical development means for children

Aims

By the end of this chapter, you should have extended your knowledge of children's physical development in the areas of motor skills, both large and fine, and of the senses (sight, hearing, touch, taste and smell). You should recognise how these link together and are interdependent. You should also understand how other aspects of development, cognitive, language and social and emotional, are intertwined with physical development and how it is necessary to consider the impact of growth in one area on any, or all, of the others. In deepening your own understanding, as a practitioner you will be able to ensure that your provision not only meets the requirements for children at whatever point they have reached physically but also presents ample challenge to move them on their own individual pathway and according to the expectations of the EYFS.

 ## Links to EYFS

- Babies and children learn by being active, and physical development takes place across all areas of learning and development.
- Plan activities that offer physical challenges and plenty of opportunities for physical activity.

- Give sufficient time for children to use a range of equipment to persist in activities, practising new and existing skills and learning from their mistakes.

- Notice and value children's natural and spontaneous movements, through which they are finding out about their bodies and exploring sensations such as balance.

- Introduce appropriate vocabulary to children, alongside their activities.

- Provide time and opportunities for children with physical disabilities or motor impairments to develop their physical skills, working in partnership with relevant specialists such as physiotherapists and occupational therapists.

(DfES 2007: 90–1)

Introduction

Traditionally, much of what we have used to understand children's physical development has depended on theories which have proposed stages and 'milestones' that structured children's developmental progress, mainly in line with medical models. This was the result of extensive research in the first half of the twentieth century, particularly by Gesell and his associates who proposed a 'maturational theory of growth and development which emphasizes maturation of the nervous system as the principal driver of the physical and motor aspects of human behavior' (Piek 2006: 25). Examples of this in use include Illingworth (1987) and Mary Sheridan's publications. Although there has been a move towards more naturalistic, multi-professional observational assessment (Gallahue and Ozmun 2006: 473), standardised materials designed to measure infant and child motor development have reflected a maturational approach. These include the Griffiths Scales, Bayley Scales of Infant Development and the Peabody Developmental Motor Scales (Piek 2006). Although the milestones they proposed have a place in assessing children, they account for 'average' development and tend to ignore what is beyond their parameters and how an infant is actually progressing. Looking out for these milestones can obscure what an infant is actually doing and can prevent a practitioner from supporting and enhancing this. Stage theories can ignore the interplay between children's natural proclivities and their environment or between children and the expectations of adults around them.

See, smell, touch (12 months)

Studying physical development in isolation has followed the practice of looking at aspects of development discretely: physical, social, language and cognition, each subdivided further. For example, physical development is usually divided into a set of sub-skills. There are a number of terms used to describe these but generally they are:

- gross or large motor skills which involve the whole body, such as walking, running or climbing;
- fine or small motor skills, such as picking up small objects, using tools or doing up buttons.

This can be useful in structuring our observations of children, but it can close our eyes to what children actually do. There are a number of activities that include aspects of both: dressing, for example, or using a spoon to pick up food then moving it towards the mouth. If children are having difficulty with any of these movements, it needs careful observation to decide which elements may need support and practice.

Although this way of structuring what we see has its place in attempting to help those who are new to the study of children's development, it can deny the complexities and exceptions to these pathways that naturally occur. For example, not all babies roll, sit up, crawl then walk in that order (see p. 23). Some miss out crawling altogether, finding other ways to get around or just moving swiftly to walking. Time frames vary greatly, due to a variety of genetically determined traits and cultural and personal preferences, but the majority of young children are successful within acceptable limits. The downside of adhering to these formalised structures, beyond thinking there may be problems when there are none, is that by dividing development into discrete areas the interdependency of one area upon another may be ignored. One example is the dependence of the child on good control of the muscles of the face for speaking, which is an interdependency often disregarded by parents and practitioners alike. For instance, children with Down syndrome generally have difficulty with muscle control, particular fine motor movements. This leads to delayed speech, because they find it hard to control the complex series of facial muscle sequences needed to produce clear speech, not because they cannot understand nor compose what they wish to say. Many other young children these days also have difficulties with speech because they fail to have sufficient practice in gaining control of the muscles required.

In considering how language and physical development interlink, it is important to think about the early skills that underpin successful language acquisition and how these interlink with physical and sensory skills. The ability to imitate (and initiate) facial expressions and sounds develops early in a baby and is shaped by adults who are 'in tune'. Barnet and Barnet (1999) name these 'language partners'. Joint attention and shared, sustained thinking is important in achieving language, so proper use of the key-worker ideal is essential so that practitioners really know their children in day care (Elfer et al. 2003). Attention and listening are skills that develop as language partners pick up on areas of interest to infants; additionally, this close relationship helps infants to filter out those events in their environment which are not important to the task in hand. Being able to ignore sensory information that is not crucial at the time helps in structuring how information is stored and subsequently used.

Brain plus body

The paragraph above illustrates how dividing up development disregards how closely brain and body are interlinked. Neither can work adequately without the other; even in situations where someone is paralysed, many of the body's internal systems continue to function. The brain is fed by the information that the body submits to it. Perception, how the world is understood, is crucial in ensuring that incoming information via the senses and movement is absorbed and processed so that the individual reacts or behaves in an appropriate way.

Physical development needs to be seen as one contributing strand to infants' holistic development. Emphasis over a number of years, both in research and education, has been on brain or cognitive development, rather than recognising how the brain is fed by physical experiences or knowledge and how understanding is accrued through physical exploration. Piaget (1955) understood this, arguing that infants in their first two years must structure their growing understanding of the world through actively exploring their environments. Although he is now thought to have underestimated babies' abilities at birth, his theories gave new impetus to research as the infants' role in the construction of their own world was recognised. Piaget's theories, therefore, still have resonance today: babies need to explore to develop; it does not just happen by chance.

Schemas

Children, like Billy in Chapter 8, often develop *schemas*. This is a term first used by Piaget (1955) and extended by Athey (2007) in the 1970s, which Gura (1996: 16) describes as:

> patterns of distinguishing features such as movement, shape, form and sound [...] Learning develops as a result of attempting to match patterns from the world outside to the schema inside our heads. As our outer world expands so our schemas become more elaborated and vice versa. The more elaborated our schema, the more complex the connections we can make between areas of experience.

Examples of schemas include lines, connection, enclosure and envelopment. As a baby not yet a year old, my grandson loved pattern and delighted in making lines; he liked to line up his bricks or to link his wooden train track together in long lines. In desperation, he would empty out the video store and line the boxes up very exactly along the floor of the sitting room (which is some 10 metres long). This improved his ability to crawl and carry, a very difficult task, as well as his dexterity in lining up his chosen items so exactly. It would have been easy to curtail these activities, especially the use of videos, but this was an important aspect of his learning and needed to be supported. By considering sometimes puzzling aspects of children's physical behaviour as part of their schema, it is possible to understand what they are doing and to extend their play. A good photographic review of schemas is provided online by the Regional Support Centre/Scotland South and West (http://www.rsc-sw-scotland.ac.uk/project_pages/docfiles/health_social_care/Photo%20Schemas.ppt).

Actions becoming automatic

Not only do the infant and child need to build up the motor and sensory knowledge and competences to enable them to feed the brain, much of what they learn to do in childhood needs to become automatic if they are to free up room for thinking about other skills which are not yet unconscious. For example, children learn to walk up and down stairs in a mature way (alternating feet on each higher step without holding on); this enables them to carry things or look over to a friend or parent while still climbing. In a familiar situation, they have learnt where their feet need to go and are confident in their balance. If, however, something intervenes to change their familiarity, perhaps a period of illness, new glasses or even new shoes, there is a period of readjustment to the new information before the process once more becomes automatic. Children, while learning to do this, will make errors which are not wilful but are part of a readjustment to the changed circumstance they have met. They also need to adjust to growth and learn that their bodies' dimensions are not the same as last week. It takes amazingly few attempts to complete this readjustment. For example, Michael, a timid four-year-old, had learnt to use the small slide in our setting over quite a long period of time but was now confident. A visit to his new nursery introduced him to a slide which was slightly higher and steeper. He was willing to try but needed support from an adult for the first few attempts until he had readjusted to the new situation. Much concern has been expressed in the past about rote learning, mainly based, it seems, on learning the times tables. This must not be confused with what a child needs to do when learning a new movement or how to use a new piece of equipment. Repetition here leads to mastery. Children who practise playing a musical instrument or climbing a slide (or perhaps, today, using the computer keyboard) do not eventually have to think about what they are doing. They free their brain and body from thinking about the notes they are playing; they are not dependent on transcribing the notes they see before their fingers can play the tune (or before they can accurately remember the sound and 'play by ear'). Once these basic patterns are learnt, they can move on to incorporating more challenging techniques into their repertoire.

The senses

In thinking about physical development, we cannot ignore the importance of the senses. Not only do we receive information through each of them, we are also guided to react physically through what they tell us. If we taste or smell some food or drink which is not fresh, these senses tell us not to carry on eating or drinking if we do not wish to be sick; if we see something dangerous coming towards us, we move quickly; if we touch something hot, we withdraw our hand. We can begin to empathise with people who have lost their sense of hearing or sight, but I was once involved with a playgroup which was preparing to admit a child who had a poor sense of touch because of an underlying skin condition. Some children do not feel pain. These are very rare conditions and thinking through the implications is stupefying. There are other disabilities that cause hypersensitivity to sensory information, especially those who have an autistic spectrum disorder (see www.optionsgroup.co.uk). In consultation with parents and from close observation, it is possible to identify difficulties and to try to avoid exposing children to experiences that cause them distress. Many young children find it hard to integrate the sensory information they receive, as Mina discovered below (see p. 35).

This indicates that no physical responses in humans are simple. In viewing motor responses to something that happens to a child, Woodfield (2004) terms the sequence of complex muscle movements 'motor strings'. This links back to the repetition needed to achieve mastery. A baby is born with a number of important reflexes, such as rooting in an attempt to find food, but most skills are acquired through the child's inner motivation to explore and learn in a supportive environment. Opportunity, practice and encouragement are the key words for what a practitioner must provide:

Practitioners must encourage the physical development of babies and young children by offering opportunities for them to learn through being active and interactive, improving their skills of coordination, control, manipulation and movement. Practitioners must support children in using all of their senses to learn about the world around them and to make connections between new information and what they already know.

(DfES 2006: 105)

Example 4

Mikey's mum moves to Scotland when he is six months old. She is lucky enough to have a choice of childcare provision and opts for a private day nursery where the practitioners care for the children well and the ratio for babies is one member of staff to two infants. Although the accommodation is limited, and there is little outside space, the children are taken out each day, and good use is made of parks and other facilities. Thought has been given to use of space, and the baby area of the large hall used by the nursery is separated from the toddler area by large, moveable, soft play blocks. Mikey settles down well and is happy with his primary caregiver at the nursery. He is already crawling when he starts and is always interested in what is happening 'over the wall'. He is quickly able to pull himself up on to the blocks to watch the older children. He is followed by another baby, slightly older, with whom he has made a close relationship. By the time he is nine months old, at his first Christmas, he has made his escape and joined the toddlers in a number of their activities. He is particularly interested in painting and, with support from the staff, manages to make handprints (and cover himself in paint!). His mother is delighted and shares his achievements at home with the nursery. At Christmas, he is able to build towers with three interlinking cups, sometimes more, and his mum is intrigued to discover that he matches the four bright colours too. By 11 months he is walking steadily and unaided. This follows the developmental pattern seen in his mother and aunt who both walked very early.

Example 5: Is seeing believing?

Mina works in a nursery where there is a group of children with language delay. She notices that the children are very dependent on their vision in the activities she provides. She is worried not only that their spoken language skills are poor but also that they are failing to use all their senses and to integrate them to gain as much information as possible about their world and to put it to good use. These difficulties really came home to her when she was using feely bags with the group. One little boy, nearly four years old, was really upset and cried when he was gently discouraged from looking into the bag rather than feeling the contents. Mina decided to use this activity to start to encourage the children to feel and describe. She started by making very large bags into which she placed large familiar toys such as trucks and dolls and let the children feel the articles from outside the bag. Gradually she moved on to feely boxes, using a variety of items, including food. Not only were the children encouraged to feel but they were also asked to describe the contents, eventually asking the questions themselves. Soon the group was able to accept blindfolds and were introduced to traditional games such as Blind Man's Bluff.

Questions

- Children's development has to be seen as 'holistic'. Debate this term with colleagues and try to agree on a definition. How will this impact on your practice?

- Think about what babies can do at birth. Discuss what your thoughts are with colleagues. What is your reaction to your findings? How will you support babies and infants now?

- Think of a child whose physical/sensory development has been problematic for you. Try to work out why this was and how you would support him or her now.

- Think about what you provide in your setting to support children's physical development. What guidance or research do you use and what should you put in place so that staff and parents know both your philosophy and practice?

As a starting point, consider the Examples above. Referring to the EYFS Practice Guidance (2008), how would you respond to these discussion points?

- effective practice;

- look, listen and note;

- planning and resourcing.

References

Athey, C. (2007) *Extending Thought in Young Children,* 2nd edn, London: Paul Chapman Publishing.

Barnet, A. B. and Barnet, R. J. (1999) *The Youngest Minds,* New York: Touchstone.

DfES (2006) *Primary National Strategy: Primary Framework for Literacy and Mathematics,* Nottingham: HSMO.

Elfer, P., Goldschmied, E. and Selleck, D. R. (2003) *Key Persons in the Nursery: Building Relationships for Quality Provision,* London: David Fulton.

Gallahue, D. L. and Ozmun, J. C. (2006) *Understanding Motor Development,* 6th edn, New York: McGraw-Hill.

Gura, P. (1996) *Resources for Early Learning: Children, Adults and Stuff,* London: Hodder & Stoughton.

Illingworth, R. S. (1987) *The Development of the Infant and Young Child,* 9th edn, Edinburgh: Churchill Livingstone.

Piaget, J. (1955) *The Child's Construction of Reality,* London: Routledge and Kegan Paul.

Piek, J. P. (2006) *Infant Motor Development,* Champaign, Ill.: Human Kinetics.

Regional Support Centre/Scotland South and West (n.d.) 'Schemas, Early Education and Child Care'. Online: www.rsc-sw-scotland.ac.uk/project_pages/docfiles/health_social_care/Photo%20Schemas.ppt.

⊞   Sharma, A. and Cockerill, H. (2008) *Mary Sheridan: From Birth to Five Years: Children's Developmental Progress,* 3rd edn, London: Routledge.

⊞   Woodfield, L. (2004) *Physical Development in the Early Years,* London: Continuum.

3 Balancing risk and challenge

Aims

At the end of this chapter, you should be able to distinguish between 'risk' and 'challenge', be able to understand the importance of recognising and reacting to this in your work with children and be able to articulate the reasons for its consideration in your workplace with colleagues and parents from a position of strength. Examples of interesting initiatives and projects from the UK and elsewhere are included throughout the chapter to provide discussion points and practical aspects which could be introduced into the settings in which you work.

 ## The EYFS principles

An overview of welfare requirements starts with:

> Children learn best when they are healthy, safe and secure, when their individual needs are met and when they have positive relationships with the adults caring for them. The welfare requirements are designed to support providers in creating a setting which is welcoming, safe and stimulating, and where children are able to enjoy themselves, to grow in confidence and to fulfil their potential.
>
> (DfES 2007b: Section 3.1: 14)

The Statutory Framework (DfES 2007a) presents these to providers as general welfare requirements: 'The provider must take necessary steps to safeguard and promote the welfare of children. The provider must promote the good health of the children, take necessary steps to prevent the spread of infection, and take appropriate action when they are ill' (DfES 2007a: Section 3.4: 19).

The EYFS, however, acknowledges that there needs to be some element of risk in the opportunities we offer children. It states that practitioners should, 'Build up children's confidence to take manageable risks in their play' (DfES 2007b: 90). It is the balance between the undertaking to promote children's welfare, a broad and multifaceted term, and to provide a 'stimulating' environment which will be debated here.

Introduction

The term 'risk' can be defined in a number of ways. First, it is used in the context of developmental risk, that is to say, there are factors, health, social or educational, which could affect the young child's ability to grow and learn optimally. This could apply to a child who is born with an illness or disability or lives in poverty. Papatheodorou (2005: 42) explores this definition of risk, giving advice on what to look for in a child's progress to counter the risks to optimal development. For the purposes of this chapter, however, it is applied to physical-safety issues which have resulted in children being overprotected and not able to learn how to deal with perceived dangers for themselves. In the words of Andrew Barnett, Director of the Calouste Gulbenkian Foundation UK:

> young people need both safeguards and opportunities. But our current concern is that through society misreading risk children face a myriad of restrictions that are intended to support them, whether imposed by zealous parents, by policy or by those interpreting it. We do not retreat from our advocacy of child protection but we recognise that keeping children safe conversely involves them taking risks so that they can learn how to assess and respond to them; children will never understand risk if society prevents them from experiencing it.
>
> (Gill 2007: 7)

Free as a bird (5 years 10 months)

This is not the first time I have written of my concerns about the situation in which the UK finds itself with regard to children's safety:

> The term 'risk' is problematic. Like a number of terms common in education it has different meanings according to the context in which it is used. 'At risk' signals that children are vulnerable and may be harmed. It is our duty as caring professionals to ensure that this harm is at least minimised if not totally prevented. We are governed by legislation and local guidance as well as by our own ethical standards. The idea of 'risk', however, can be seen in a much more positive light if we replace it with 'challenge.' If we remove 'challenge' from children's lives it can also remove motivation and a sense of personal

achievement in overcoming challenges. It also can mean that we are not helped to manage this form of risk for ourselves, leading to a reduced ability to foresee dangers and protect ourselves.

(Nurse 2007: 124)

Today's context

Placed in a historical context, safety issues have changed, but life is probably no less secure for children than it was fifty or 150 years ago. 'Incidences of child abduction and murder, although tragic, are extremely rare and have remained largely unchanged in the last fifty years' (Tovey 2007: 3). Tovey adds that it is the fear of danger that has resulted in overprotection and restrictions on children's play, even though accidents in the home are far more likely to occur. Admittedly there are some new hazards, from increased traffic, widespread internet use and drug addiction (leading, perhaps, at the time this is written, to tragic cases involving extreme violence), and these need the input of adults who are committed to eradicating these dangers, rather than reinforcing them, and enabling children to learn how to protect themselves. Illness and disease in the developed world have decreased remarkably and those that remain are increasingly countered by scientific research. Children are safeguarded from hazardous workplaces for longer and longer in their lives and, despite the periodic abuse cases covered in detail in the media, are probably much safer from abusers than in earlier times. Of course, children who are born elsewhere in the world do not have the advantages of a safe and secure environment. Millions of children face absolute poverty, disease and war, and some of these children who will attend our settings come to the UK to escape horrors we can only partly imagine.

The EYFS is in the spirit of trying to return some of the children's childhood to them, but it hedges its bets. The best that practitioners can achieve is to avoid making it prescriptive and turning it into a checklist that inhibits children's natural interests and play.

The legal position

Whatever practitioners provide, however, must adhere to current legislation, not only to protect the children but also to safeguard the practitioners themselves. The EYFS is clear on this: 'The statutory framework sets out the legal requirements which cover safeguarding and ensuring children's welfare, staff, premises, environment and equipment, organisation, documentation and reporting. It also contains statutory guidance which providers must take into account when seeking to fulfil the legal requirements' (DfES 2007b: Section 3.2: 14).

There is an increasing concern, however, about the current legislation and how it can stand in the way of offering children excitement and challenge. In 2002, the Play Safety Forum published *Managing Risk in Play Provision,* a position statement which brought together thinking from a number of national organisations involved in children's play. The Health and Safety Executive (HSE) response to this was perhaps indicative of a change towards safety issues. With reference to this document, it stated:

> It articulates the balance between the benefit and the need for children to play against the duty of play providers to provide safe play. It makes clear that the safety must be considered at all stages of play provision but that, inevitably, there will be risk of injury when children play, as there is risk of injury in life generally. We must not lose sight of the important developmental role of play for children in the pursuit of the unachievable goal of absolute safety. The important message is though that there must be freedom from unacceptable risk of life-threatening or permanently disabling injury in play.
>
> (http://www.hse.gov.uk/foi/internalops/sectors/
> cactus/5_02_15.pdf, p. 4)

This is a very different approach from that encountered by a head teacher of a nursery school I know who was once told by her local HSE, after a child had cracked his wrist in a minor fall, that no climbing apparatus could be more than 15 centimetres from the ground. Government has now generally accepted that preventing all physical risk is impossible and that an unforeseen consequence could be that current legislation impairs a child's ability to learn to care for himself. Gill (2007: 21–3) provides an overview of changing thinking, highlighting the HSE's 'Get a Life' campaign, inaugurated in 2006. Bill Callaghan, Chair of the Health and Safety Commission, launched this saying, 'sensible risk management is emphatically about saving lives, not stopping them' (http://www.hse.gov.uk/risk/statement.htm, 2006). The Better Regulations Commission (BRC, replaced in January 2008 by the Risk and Regulation Advisory Council, RRAC) considers 'our national attitude to risk is becoming defensive and disproportionate' (BRC 2008a). In its publication, *Public Risk: The Next Frontier for Better Regulation* (2008b), the BRC highlights childhood obesity, shifting roles in health care and child safety as concerns to be addressed.

Until all these concerns are reconsidered, however, practitioners are bound by the legislation in place, though this allows for a certain amount of discretion if policies are in place and understood by all concerned. Wrapping children in cotton wool does not help them to develop strongly and leads them to take risks they might not be able to cope with as they grow older. The Pre-school Learning Alliance (PLA) provides thorough guidance, including links to the relevant legislation and examples of risk assessment forms. It counsels:

> There is quite rightly much emphasis on keeping children safe in early years settings with a duty to minimise risk in all situations. However, children need and instinctively want to be able to take risks in order that they can test their abilities and strengths. What better environment for them to do so than that of an early years setting where practitioners will already have removed hazards not readily identifiable to young children and will provide well managed opportunities for appropriate 'risk taking' to take place, for example, climbing to the top of the climbing frame, building a very tall tower of bricks and then knocking it down, or simply climbing the stairs. Children need support to take these risks as part of their learning and development.
>
> (http://seye.pre-school.org.uk/tour/189, Section 5)

Hodgkinson (2008) in a tongue-in-cheek article for the *Daily Telegraph,* celebrates the idea of inactive parenting: standing back and letting children be. He stipulates, however, 'Clearly we don't let our children jump out of windows or go about with unchanged nappies. There is carefree and there is careless, and there is a difference.'

Some other models

How practitioners start to rethink what is available in their settings to encourage challenge depends on an understanding of what children need and a commitment to promoting and providing it. There are several different models which practitioners can view in deciding how to develop their own ideas. It is rarely good practice to try to adopt a whole approach from a different cultural context, but elements from each can be considered and used to create something new and appropriate. Both Reggio Emilia and High/Scope readily admit that they adopted elements from elsewhere into their own philosophies.

Scandinavian childhoods are often evoked as exemplars of the optimal childhood experience. Wagner (2006), an American, has compared Nordic childhoods with the American version (similar to ours?) and has explored the idea of a *good childhood* and intercultural differences in adults' beliefs about children's rights and their place in society. Drawing on her own experiences and those of the Scandinavian authors who have contributed to her book, Wagner postulates that:

> Nordic people espouse that children and adults are equal along many planes. They enact this principle through their commitment to emancipation, that is, the notion that children should be free from excessive adult control and supervision [...] They spend a great deal of time (*again by my American calibrations*) in free play, often beyond the immediate supervision of adults, running indoors and out as their interests dictate, and engaging in potentially dangerous (*to my American eyes*) activities [...] such as climbing trees or using sharp knives and adult power tools.
>
> (Wagner 2006: 292)

Yet few accidents occur, reflecting the experience in Reggio Emilia where children are taught to handle potentially dangerous materials, such as broken glass, through proper use of safety equipment and are left alone then to take responsibility for their own safety. Wagner retells (2006: 289) the occasion when she saw ten toddlers in snowsuits, not yet three years old, waiting for a train to take them to a forest pre-school. Although teachers were close by, they were not overly anxious. As a nursery teacher, I can remember my anguish in taking children on trips out of the relatively secure setting of the school. I started counting the children when we left and did not stop until we had them all safely back...yet the few accidents we had occurred in the classroom, not beyond it. The Scandinavian experience does not stem from lax standards, rather from the differing expectations of children's capabilities and an understanding of how their world works. Following from the Scandinavian experience, one of the most exciting developments to reach the UK has been the Forest Schools projects which address so many of the concerns raised about over-protectiveness in the UK today. Forest schools originated in Sweden but arrived in the UK in the mid-1990s via Denmark, introduced by Bridgewater College. Forest School initiatives now cover the country but have had particular success in Wales where they are supported by the Forestry Commission. Forest Schools have a set of aims which are designed to counteract some of the concerns about children's development in the UK today. Shropshire County Council (online) includes these:

> Forest School is particularly successful in developing self-esteem and confidence and motivating children who, for a range of reasons, struggle in a classroom environment.
>
> Forest School has additional physical, social and health benefits for children and young people who are leading increasingly indoor lives, helping them to enjoy physical activity outdoors and mitigate obesity.

Programmes are designed for children from the age of three and include a variety of experiences outdoors which engage children in physical activities and enable them to increase their ability to cope with risk and problem-solving, working together with others to achieve success. Examples of what young children do includes building shelters, finding mini-beasts, hide and seek and playing in a natural environment. Jumping into mud pools seems to be a favourite. Those who work with the children are trained explicitly in the strategies developed to promote these open-air schools. Programmes are now being evaluated by O'Brien and Murray (2006) for the Forestry Commission. They linked the Forest School experience firmly to Every Child Matters' five outcomes and concluded:

> The Campaign for Adventure (Lewis 2005) is concerned about the current climate of risk aversion and advocates seeing the positive side of risk, for example when children test their skills and learn to face new challenges. Forest School demonstrates that effective measures can be taken to reduce and manage risk to an acceptable standard [...] The government [...] is now encouraging a greater emphasis on the use of the outdoors for learning: *'Outdoor education gives depth to the curriculum and makes an important contribution to students' physical, personal and social education'*
>
> (Office for Standards in Education [Ofsted] 2004: 2)

Within the UK, Playlink and the Free Play Network, amongst others, have worked to improve children's opportunities for physical play. Wales in particular has produced policies that support this. Beacon (2008) provides a brief overview of the new Welsh approach to learning through play in the primary school, and more details can be found on the Welsh government website. In summary, practitioners are urged to reflect and rethink what the consequences are if we do not offer children what they need. It is very difficult to predict the future (my teachers fifty years ago could not have foreseen the changes I have experienced in my life – the insular, black-and-white 1950s' childhood turned into glorious global Technicolor). Children will need to be resilient, adaptable, flexible and questioning to succeed in a world that becomes ever-more complex. Practitioners sometimes need to take risks themselves. A last quote, food for thought and debate:

> At the Lumiar School in São Paulo, two little boys are enthusiastically testing the boundaries between self-expression and anarchy by lobbing building blocks into an oversize doll's house. As a grown-up wanders over to make sure no one is getting hurt, three-year-old Rafael grabs the wall of the house and tries to haul it to the ground.
>
> 'Careful!' shouts teacher Christiane Checchia.
>
> 'But I want to pull it down', pleads Rafael.
>
> 'Hold on then', says Checchia, 'I'll help you' – and together they grab hold of the wall and tear it to the ground.
>
> At Lumiar, it is not uncommon to see teachers tearing down walls, throwing things around or jumping around the corridors pretending to be characters from *Star Wars*.
>
> Ricardo Semler, who established the Lumiar School, states: 'We are trying to prove that by giving kids freedom, they will in the end be better educated.'
>
> (*Daily Telegraph*, 9 February 2004)

Example 6: Making the best of what you have

Allkids Primary School was sited on the borders between an affluent and disadvantaged area in the inner city and admitted children from both ends of the social spectrum to its nursery unit. The children also came from a multitude of ethnic, religious and language backgrounds. They all shared, however, a restricted physical experience in that the area contained few outside areas, such as parks and woods, which they could visit, and few had gardens. The whole area was considered too unsafe to allow children outside without adult supervision not only because of the traffic but also because of the numbers of people passing through it to work or en route to somewhere else. The teacher and nursery nurse were concerned about their children's lack of physical experience from their observations and determined to do something to improve the situation. For example, they had a number of three-year-olds, living in small flats where they had no access to stairs and who went every-where in pushchairs. In preparation, they audited the materials and accom-modation they had, researched the whole area of physical education and detailed children's existing range of physical skills through their observations. As a result, and with the agreement of the school and local education authority inspectors and local Health and Safety advisers, they were able to use the very high ceilings in this Victorian school to construct a mezzanine floor, reached by a staircase, which was intended for use as the home and role-play area. This was to become the children's own, into which adults were invited rather than having a right of access. This followed on from the team's research into Reggio Emilia's provision for children's spaces, not overlooked by staff. The other area of development was outside. The nursery unit had already a good sized outside play space, adequate for wheeled toys, sand and water play and ball games but, like many, it was flat and uninteresting and suffered from over-use of the bikes and trikes and boys with lots of energy to diffuse. Its organisation and use were revisited, and the idea of the 'outside class-room' was incorporated into the planning, as well as creating areas for growing and quiet contemplation. The outside area had, however, been split into two, probably because of a significant slope. The part with the slope, more than half of the space available, was hidden behind a high wall and was only accessible though a solid, locked, doorway. Beyond, a wild garden had developed over the years with a variety of trees, bushes, plants and wildlife. The team decided to open this to the children, following the example set by the Forest Schools development in the UK. Much of it was left as it was: with the help of the Parks Department in the area, plants were checked, with those dangerous to children removed, and paths were uncovered. Otherwise the area was untouched. New equipment was needed to support these devel-opments, such as tools and suitable clothing. Funding for this was initially provided from the school's budget but later from donations and fundraising.

The project was not without its critics. Censure and disquiet met the team at first, both from parents and from within the school. Most of this reflected health and safety concerns, but there was also some concern about play and lack of formal teaching. However, as the team members had researched what they were doing thoroughly, each was able to explain and illustrate the benefits for children from their knowledge of the reading and other models. Workshops and open sessions were held in the unit and, gradually, as progress could be seen in the children's development – and no serious accidents occurred – everyone began to see how worthwhile the changes had been.

One insurmountable problem appeared at first. To give the children access during the day to all three areas, each needed an adult present to ensure that school and local authority guidelines were met. Sometimes a classroom assistant could be released, but this was inconsistent. So, in the beginning, it proved impossible to maintain this, and it was mainly the wild-garden aspect that was restricted. The difficulty with staffing in the end resolved itself as the school moved to incorporating the two reception classes into the new early years unit in preparation for the EYFS. This released four more team members – teachers and classroom assistants – to work with the children and this was successful.

Example 7: Taking a risk and succeeding

Kati is a bright little girl, just five years old, who has cerebral palsy. This affects her general movement and also her speech, though she has learnt to walk without aids and is understandable to those who know her well. She is very determined and wants to join in fully with the children who also attend the mainstream foundation-stage class she attends at her local school. The nursery team were acutely aware that allowing Kati to do what she wanted incurred elements of risk. With her parents' help, the staff of the school have researched the nature of her disability and have stopped being over-protective. They have also discussed with the children why Kati has some difficulties and how they can all help her, without doing everything for her. In circle time, Kati has been given the opportunity to express how she sees herself in relation to her peers and what she would like them to do to support her. The staff has learnt through observation what Kati can do for herself and what she can do with help. Planning carefully reflects this, and the practitioners discuss, with Kati and her parents as well as the language therapists and physiotherapists overseeing her development, what to aim for next. They are concerned that Kati should achieve her ultimate goal successfully and plan for this through developing a series of small steps that build up to the finale. These small steps enable her to practise what she needs to do securely and in a play situation. For example, now that she is in the final year of the foundation stage, Kati is determined that she will, like the others, go up to collect her lunch from the cooks, see what is available, choose for herself and then carry her plate back to her place.

Questions

- Reflect on your own childhood and recall incidents when you enjoyed life to the full. Share these with friends and colleagues, especially those who are younger or older than you. How does this link with what you provide for the children in your setting?

- What are your greatest anxieties in considering risk and challenge? Have you ever needed to deal with a parent who was not happy with your provision or where a child had had an injury? How did you resolve this and what did you learn that is relevant to your work with children today?

- Audit the provision you have for physical development. Does this meet all children's needs? How can you incorporate challenge and how can you be sure that all ages and abilities are catered for?

- How do you now perceive risk? How can you make this manageable? Draw up guidelines for your staff that match both the legislation you must work towards yet do not remove the element of challenge from your provision.

As a starting point, consider the examples above. Referring to the EYFS Practice Guidance (2008), how would you respond to these discussion points?

- effective practice;

- look, listen and note;

- planning and resourcing.

References

Barnett, A. (2007) 'Preface' to T. Gill (2007) *No Fear: Growing Up in a Risk Averse Society,* London: Calouste Gulbenkian Foundation.

Beacon, A. (2008) 'Time to Play in Wales', *Report,* May.

Better Regulation Commission (BRC) (2008a) *Risk, Responsibility, Regulation: Whose Risk Is It Anyway?* Available online at http://archive.cabinetoffice.gov.uk/brc/publications/risk_report.html.

BRC (2008b) *Public Risk: The Next Frontier for Better Regulation.* Available online at http://archive.cabinetoffice.gov.uk/brc/upload/assets/www.brc.gov.uk/public_risk_report_070108.pdf.

DfES (2007a) *Statutory Framework for the Early Years Foundation Stage,* London: DfES.

DfES (2007b) *Practice Guidance for the Early Years Foundation Stage,* London: DfES.

Gill, T. (2007) *No Fear: Growing Up in a Risk Averse Society,* London: Calouste Gulbenkian Foundation.

Hodgkinson, T. (2008) 'Idle Parenting Means Happy Children', *Daily Telegraph,* 16 February.

Lewis, I. (2005) 'Nature and Adventure', *ECOS,* 1: 14–19.

Nurse, A. D. (2007) *The New Early Years Professional: Dilemmas and Debates,* London: David Fulton/Routledge.

O'Brien, L. and Murray, R. (2006) *A Marvellous Opportunity for Children to Learn: A Participatory Evaluation of Forest School in England and Wales,* Norwich: HMSO.

Ofsted (2004) *Outdoor Education: Aspects of Good Practice,* London: Ofsted.

Papatheodorou, T. (2005) 'Play and Special Needs', in J. Moyles (ed.) *The Excellence of Play,* 2nd edn, Maidenhead: Open University Press.

Play Safety Forum (2002) *Managing Risk in Play Provision: a Position Statement,* London: National Children's Bureau/Children's Play Council/Sutcliffe Play.

Pre-school Learning Alliance (n.d.) *Safe Early Years Environments: A Practitioner's Guide.* Available online at seye.pre-school.org.uk (accessed 3 June 2008).

Tovey, H. (2007) *Playing Outdoors: Spaces and Places: Risks and Challenges,* Maidenhead: Open University Press.

Wagner, J. and Einarsdottir, J. (eds) (2006) *Nordic Childhoods and Early Education,* Greenwich, Conn.: Information Age Publishing.

Thinking about movement and space

Aims

By the end of this chapter, you will recognise that infants and children are continually moving and testing themselves out physically in their environment as they grow. You should be able to recognise the importance of movement as the basis of other developmental aspects, such as cognitive development, that form part of a child's growth towards maturity. You will understand how important movement is to a sense of self and confidence, as well as to health and well-being. You will be able to reflect on the ways you already support this in your setting and consider how to develop it further to provide appropriate experiences and challenge. You will understand the need to offer full access to all the children in your provision, taking account of the resources you have both in your setting and beyond. In your role as an advocate, you will be asked to consider how space is used in your community to support children. The following chapter links closely to the EYFS and will help you put this aspect into practice.

Introduction

The importance of the relationship between movement learning and all other aspects of children's early learning is based on the evidence that young children use movement as the medium to explore and investigate the world around them. Without efficient movement ability, this exploration may be hampered and children's learning experiences, in a whole range of environments, may be more limited than it ought to be. A key responsibility therefore, for all those who care for and educate young children, is to ensure that the fundamental motor patterns, so essential to successful learning and to enabling children to reach their full potential as movers, are established and secured.

(Maude 2004)

I sit at the back of a reception class, containing a number of little children many still four years old. The classroom is not at all large and an odd L-shape. There is a place for each child, so the space is almost entirely taken up by tables and chairs. The class is crowded on to the carpet at the teacher's feet. She has her daily lesson plan by her and is desperately trying to fit everything that she intended to do in the time slot allocated for it. Part of her time has been taken up by assembly and the children have already been sitting for a long period. The teacher and her assistant have struggled to keep them still and quiet in the hall and are continuing to do so now. I am uncomfortable on my little chair; how painful it must be for the children. I am here to see a particular child whose delayed development is causing concern, but my interests are consumed by what is happening here (and in many other similar situations across the country). The more the children wiggle, the longer it takes for the lesson objectives to be reached. This is not the teacher's fault. She is part of a system that says one thing then expects another when the inspection team arrives. Children should not be expected to sit still like this for so long, because usually they cannot. I become obsessed by this. When are children able to sit comfortably cross-legged? I know in many other societies it is the norm for both adults and children but find little reference to it either in my textbooks or on the Internet. There was, however, one interesting comment I found:

'I spoke to some nursery children and talked to them about story time and said to them 'you really enjoy story time?' and they said 'yes we do, but the teacher likes it better than we do!' I said, 'oh why's that?' she said, 'but don't tell her, because she thinks we really really like it!' And I said 'so what's the problem?' she said 'we've got to sit cross legged and it really hurts our legs and after a while we can't concentrate', and it's something really simple, but if nursery children can tell us, we can learn from them, let their voice be heard and we can learn from them.

(Robinson 2007)

Small children have been expected to spend longer and longer periods each day in positions which are uncomfortable for them. Why do we never ask them how they feel? It is a question waiting to be answered. Although we are beginning to see changes with the introduction of the EYFS, there are years of developmentally poor practice which still need to be addressed and reworked. The knowledge about movement and freedom to move that practitioners held twenty or thirty years ago has now to be reinserted into the system. This knowledge is not new. Margaret McMillan recognised it

This is a challenge (2 years 4 months)

when she set up her nursery provision in the early years of the twentieth century:

> Children want space at all ages. But from the ages of one to seven, that is ample space, is almost as much wanted as food and air. To move, to run, to find things out by new movement, to feel one's life in every limb, that is the life of early childhood.
>
> (McMillan 1930: 10–11)

Motor and movement

The early years are exciting times for 'exploring the vast range of movement experiences available [...] for discovering that trial and error lead to success, for repeating and practising until new movement patterns are mastered and for seeking out and meeting new challenges' (Maude 2004).

Movement includes all those actions that involve the whole body, such as reaching, crawling, walking, jumping, kicking, running and skipping. It involves controlling the body in space and being aware that others are sharing that space too. It therefore includes attention and listening as well as problem-solving. Good movement has a number of prerequisites which children need to develop and practise: they need, for example, to be fit, able to balance, stable and coordinated. Movement can be spontaneous, or it can be contained and channelled as in gymnastics and dance. It can be in response to stimuli such as music or animal movements and can be used to act out a drama or mime.

Chapter 2 offered an overview of physical development and the idea of gross and fine motor skills. The terms 'motor' and movement are often used interchangeably but in working out what needs to be done to support children's development, a finer distinction is helpful. Movement is the end result, bringing all those motor skills together to perform an action or make a response physically. We are not generally aware of the series of motor skills we use in smoothly reaching for something or jumping off a wall, but these motor sequences (motor strings) have been practised time and time again until they are perfected. Woodfield (2004: 44), in her discussion on the difference between motor and movement, gives the example of the series of actions in reaching: 'When several impulses travel to several muscles (a motor string) almost like an electrical chain reaction – shoulder, upper arm, forearm, wrist and hand – a reaching movement is carried out.

Several joined mini-moves take place in this reaching; reaching is an example of a movement pattern.'

She relates these complex movement patterns to programming a computerised robot to kick and the number of individual instructions that would be needed to build up to this movement pattern, yet notes that in a human infant faced with a ball, this response would be instantaneous and unconscious. This organisation of motor skills into movement patterns is normally automatic in the right circumstances. Occasionally things go amiss, and a sensitive practitioner will be quick to spot these. A child with cerebral palsy experiences damage to motor areas in the brain before or at the time of birth. This makes it difficult, if not impossible, to make the neural connections that allow for easy physical movement. Sometimes, with appropriate therapy, other areas of the brain can take over if there has been an injury. In Kati's case (see p. 49), a small-steps approach towards a movement pattern, with plenty of practice, allowed her to achieve her goals. Children with Down syndrome tend to have hypotonia (poor muscle tone), a condition where the muscles are floppy and so movement is more difficult. Physiotherapy and early intervention programmes can help; however, good access to all the movement activities enjoyed by children of a similar age – and encouragement to join in – is crucial. Though this is a generalisation, I have met a number of small children with Down syndrome who have been quite happy to play 'baby' in the home corner all day and be pushed around in a pushchair. Encouragement to do other things was necessary with an explanation to peers that everyone needed a turn to be baby.

Play and space

How are children going to do this, and how do they achieve so much in a relatively short period of time? Information from research and literature all stress how central movement is in developing optimally. The body and brain cannot be separated in young children's learning. Children are programmed to move; this is how they find out about their world and how they prepare their bodies for finding out more throughout their lives. Before birth, babies move in the womb: they suck, swallow, kick, step and reach out. Piek (2006: 13–14) suggests these movements prepare the skeletal system for later and also start to shape the central nervous system. Some reflexes, such as stepping, which were thought to have no real purpose, are now considered to be precursors to later movement patterns. Babies also respond prenatally to external stimuli, especially sound and music, which they continue to recognise after they are born.

Throughout this book, references to play have been mainly implicit, but it is necessary to reflect on the aspects of 'play' which are important and relevant to physical development. The term 'play' is given to a variety of concepts, moving from the opposite of 'work' (thus undermining its value) to the major vehicle for children's learning. Bruce (2001: 30) presents *The 12 Features of Play* which explore current perspectives on the purpose of play. An important point she makes is that 'children choose to play. They cannot be made to play'. She also points out there are different cultural views about play and this must be born in mind when working with parents from a wide variety of backgrounds. Bruce has always compared 'free-flow play' with more structured forms which are used to support more formal learning. She never visualises this as a free-for-all; rather, she tries to capture those childhood moments, adult-free, when all elements of play come together. The question for me then arises, is structured play, which is adult-initiated, really 'play' at all? Swarbrick (2007: 107) draws together theories about play, concluding that it is 'a complex area of academic debate'. Practitioners need to consider their own views on play carefully, so that they are able to support it, not only for the children but with parents and colleagues too.

Play allows children to re-enact everyday experiences and to take risks; small children imitate what their parents, older siblings and teachers do. They pretend to drive cars, fly aeroplanes, cook and clean. Observing children closely, it is possible to see how carefully they copy what they have seen and then bring in other knowledge – gleaned from goodness knows where – to create a complex event.

For example, a group of three- and four-year-olds are in the garden, recreating a visit to a motor race. A circuit is evident and the boys race around it, driving their cars fast. Grumbling from the girls, allocated the onlookers' role, goes unheard so they work to enliven the proceedings. An 'accident' is arranged, and the girls proceed to deal with this. They arrive fast by ambulance, treat the injuries and carry the victim away (literally) to hospital, making him perform all sorts of movements to ensure his body and limbs are still working.

This spontaneous play was child-initiated and needed very few props, other than the space to do it. Several examples of movement occurred from running fast and steering at the same time to picking up and carrying the injured to the trolley (make-do stretcher). The children were capable of doing this, so no adult interfered. Despite what adults think, most children, even toddlers, know the limits to what they can do. A careful eye and patience can ensure that children challenge themselves. If the response children receive from adults is positive and not fearful, then children's confidence will grow. As the Scottish documentation states:

> Children's physical development is influenced by their growing confidence and enjoyment of physical play, by their increasing ability to control their own bodies through movement and by their physical well-being and strength. As children develop, they become faster, stronger, more mobile and more sure of their balance, and they start to use these skills in a wider range of physical activities.
> (Scottish Consultative Council on the Curriculum 2001: Section 2: 36)

Space

Children, in learning to use their bodies, instinctively know where they are and what they need to do. Practitioners can observe in general what they can do to support the group's needs but cannot be with every individual all of the time. What they need to do is provide the time and space for this developmental process to occur naturally. Bailey and Pickup (2007: 91) echo Margaret McMillan's words in advising 'A large, well-designed space that makes use of surrounding natural environments not only enlarges the scope for movement but can provide varied stimuli for movement to draw on'.

Sometimes it is not possible for the space to be 'well-designed'. Many practitioners have to make the best of what they have. Access to good outside areas may be limited and extra time to use shared space non-negotiable. There is always an opportunity, however, to create space inside. My advice to the teacher in the story that opened this chapter was to remove a number of tables and chairs to produce space (as well as seriously restricting time spent sitting on the carpet). At first this suggestion has often been met with horror – children like their own place at a table – but improved behaviour, fewer squabbles and less bad temper have usually proved the point. Babies need to move, too. Luckily, the days when playpens were prevalent are disappearing, but safety issues can override the need to be free, with babies spending too long in chairs and cots. Children need space.

One approach to thinking about space in a limited environment is to provide 'movement corners'. These are being developed through the Jabadao

Developmental Movement Play Project (2006–8) in a number of settings in Kirklees. Movement corners, like book or home corners, offer children space, normally permanent, stocked with equipment such as throws, cushions and soft blocks, 'which children can access most of the time, where they can initiate their own movement, play alone, with another child or with an adult, when they want […] it is a space where children can move spontaneously and drive the learning that their bodies need to develop functioning' (Jabadao/Children's Fund Kirklees 2007: 8). Through this project, practitioners are rethinking their approaches to providing space and appropriate strategies for children. Activities are placed on the floor rather than on a table and children find their own way to sit or lie down at storytime 'because they listen more when they are comfortable' (Jabadao/ Children's Fund Kirklees 2007: 9). The Interactive whiteboard is used to show video-clips of children moving so that they can watch themselves and comment (Jabadao/Children's Fund Kirklees 2007: 19).

Parents

Important to the success of these initiatives is the understanding and commitment of parents in continuing to support these beyond the setting. Finding activities that children and adults can share happily is essential; otherwise children will sense this is happening under duress. Practitioners, if they are asked to give advice, also need to be aware that many activities cost money which parents may not have to spare. Tina (see p. 11) used her small back garden to support her son's physical activities, but many families will not have even that. As part of the resources amassed to support parents, an audit of the area and the opportunities for parents and children to find shared activities is a starting point and outings to such places can initially be led by the setting to involve those who may be wary. Parents are beginning to develop resources of their own. One of these is a series of adventure walks around London (Jones and Lewis 2008), which could be used as a model for walks in other areas.

Urban considerations

Many of the children and families with whom we work, particularly in children's centres, will live in the heart of towns and cities in the UK where usually little thought has been given to providing interesting, safe environments for the very young (or for adolescents). Moss and Petrie (2002: 106) explore the concept of children's spaces, not just as 'physical environments certainly, but also as social, cultural and discursive'. Moss and Petrie do not prescribe what a 'children's space' should be; rather, they open up the debate by offering points for discussion:

> They are spaces of many possibilities, some predetermined but many others not, and for realising many potentials. They are spaces for processes and relationships, not primarily for the production of prespecified outcomes. They are places where children are allowed to manage risk and escape from adult anxieties, where, if they wish, free from adult gaze, they can lead their own cultural lives.
>
> (Moss and Petrie 2002: 106–7)

Although it starts with an illustration from an adventure playground in Wales, Moss and Petrie's book refers to the example of Reggio Emilia and its attitude towards young children's physical environment. In the Reggio centres, much rests not only on what they understand children need but also on understanding and respecting individual children's wishes. After a visit to Reggio, I wrote: 'Knowledge and perhaps memories of the precious moments of childhood are recognized in the creation of hidden places where children can go to imagine and converse secretly with favoured friends' (Nurse 2001: 63).

This commitment to providing 'children's spaces' differs dramatically from what is usually on offer in the UK. A couple of years ago, we were touring the English Midlands and became lost. We had turned left on to a road that did not appear on our ancient map and had entered a vast new, private, housing estate. The houses were neat with small gardens at the back but communal grass at the front. There was no physical heart to this large community. Eventually, we came across the 'centre', which comprised a multipurpose shop, a village hall and a bus stop. This was the middle of August, but there were very few children or adults around. Occasionally we saw small groups of young teenagers chatting together. Set in a 'greenfield site' a long way away from a town, there was a sense of ennui and almost of desolation although the estate was pristine. Eventually we found our way out, by the same road we had entered which was the only access road into the estate as far as we could see. The contrast between this newly built estate and the lively villages and towns we visited was marked. Who were the planners who had seemingly paid so little attention to the needs of children and families in building this and countless similar housing projects across the country?

In the UK, those who plan and construct new housing, whether in the public or private sector, have seemed to pay little attention to the needs of children and young people who may live there. This is in contradiction to the care that other European countries take in creating space within communities for children's play. The Free Play Network/Playlink website provides an exhibition of photographs from places here and abroad, both despairing and exciting. Look at these and reflect on the possibilities. (See www.freeplaynetwork.org.uk/playlink/exhibition/woepossibility.)

Questions

- What kinds of activity do the children in your setting enjoy if left to their own devices? Look at what individuals are doing and then how children of the same age or phase use space. Discuss what you have seen with colleagues and parents.

- Revisit theories about play in the context of movement. Try to clarify your understanding and philosophy of play, then debate this with colleagues. Are there other ways of describing play which ensure that it is not undervalued and its role in development misunderstood?

- How is the space in your setting used? What are your priorities if space is limited? Reflect on your views and see if they have changed. How could you now alter your accommodation to meet children's need for space?

- How do you encourage parents to play a greater part in supporting their children's movement experience? What resources could you put together to support them?

References

Bailey, R. and Pickup, I. (2007) 'Movement Learning: Bringing Movement into the Classroom', in R. Austin (ed.) (2007) *Letting the Outside in: Developing Teaching and Learning Beyond the Early Years Classroom,* Stoke-on-Trent: Trentham.

Bruce, T. (2001) *Learning through Play: Babies, Toddlers and the Foundation Years,* London: Hodder & Stoughton.

Jones, B. and Lewis, C. (2008) *Adventure Walks for Families,* London: Frances Lincoln.

Maude, P. (2004) 'To Examine the Implications of Enhancing Movement Observation and Analysis Skills in Order to Make a Difference to the Motor Development of Children Aged 3–7 Years', Canterbury Christ Church University, SpinEd Project.

Children's Fund Kirklees 2006–8 (2007) *Developmental Movement Play Project: Interim Report February 2007,* Leeds: Jabadao, National Centre for Movement, Learning and Health.

McMillan, M. (1930) *The Nursery School,* 2nd edn, London: Dent & Sons. Available online at http://core.roehampton.ac.uk/digital/froarc/mcmnur/index.htm (accessed 8 July 2008).

Moss, P. and Petrie, P. (2002) *From Children's Services to Children's Spaces,* London: RoutledgeFalmer.

Nurse, A. (2001) 'A Question of Inclusion', in L. Abbott and C. Nutbrown (eds) *Experiencing Reggio Emilia; Implications for Pre-School Practice,* Buckingham: Open University Press.

Piek, J. (2006) *Infant Motor Development,* Champaign, Ill.: Human Kinetics.

Robinson, C. (2007) 'Learner Voice', Harnessing Technology: BECTA Research forum 2007, 17 September, London: Royal Society for the Arts.

Scottish Consultative Council on the Curriculum (2001) *A Curriculum Framework for Children 3 to 5,* Dundee: Learning and Teaching Scotland.

Swarbrick, N. (2007) 'Play and Its Role in Early Learning', in M. Wild and H. Mitchell (eds), *Early Childhood Studies: Reflective Reader,* Exeter: Learning Matters.

Woodfield, L. (2004) *Physical Development in the Early Years,* London: Continuum.

5 Movement and space in practice

 The EYFS principles

Movement and space is how children learn to move with confidence, imagination and safety, with an awareness of space, themselves and others (DfES 2007b: 90–1).

Babies and children learn by being active, and physical development takes place across all areas of learning and development.

Practitioners are expected to:

- Motivate children to be active and help them develop movement skills through praise, encouragement, games and appropriate guidance.
- Notice and value children's natural and spontaneous movement skills through praise, encouragement, games and appropriate guidance.
- Allow sufficient space, indoors and outdoors, to set up relevant activities for energetic play.

The EYFS offers developmental points for each age phase. Scenarios provide ideas in context and additional activities are suggested below. Resources to support the practitioner or the family are included at the end of this chapter. The information here should be cross-referenced to the practical guidance offered by the EYFS documentation.

From birth–11 months

Development matters

- Make movements with arms and legs which gradually become more controlled.
- Use movement and sensory exploration to link up with their immediate movement.

Key words

contact, comfort, rapid change, sensory integration

From 8–20 months

Development matters

- Make strong and purposeful movements, often moving from the position in which they are placed.
- Use their increasing mobility to connect with toys, objects and people.
- Show delight in the freedom and changing perspectives that standing or beginning to walk brings.

Key words

developing control, purposeful, mobility, awareness

Scenario 1

Beni is three months old and looked after by a childminder three days a week while his mother works. He has been with Anna since he was six weeks old. Anna also looks after an older baby, Shari, who is nearly a year old. Her ground-floor flat is spacious, and she has access to a large garden, which she uses as often as possible. Beni is learning to reach for things and,

Ready, steady, go (3 years 9 months)

every time he spends a day with Anna, she notices how rapidly he is developing. He often now manages to bring his hands in front of his face and will stare at them for several seconds. Anna has a stock of mobiles she has made from different materials. She has used different colours and textures and some make noises too. She alternates these, placing them about 25 centimetres away from him; he will watch these intently and occasionally reach out towards them. She is fascinated to see that he is starting to kick out at the mobile, realising it moves when he touches it. When placed on his tummy, he lifts his head and follows Anna as she moves around near him. He is also captivated by Shari who has just begun to walk and will point at Beni and smile. She has just learnt to call him 'baby' and is really pleased when Anna responds and repeats it back to her. Shari gives toys to Beni (though they have often been sucked first and Anna is quick to ensure that they are clean) and he follows her intently. Like Shari, Beni's favourite pastime when he is awake is to play with Anna. He likes to be held, and Anna will jiggle him on her knee or lift him high in the air. He smiles and coos when he is pleased and Anna turns this into a game that involves Shari as well. Outside, Shari is becoming used to walking on the different surfaces: grass, earth and pavement. She pushes Anna away now when she feels confident; though she often goes 'bumpsadaisy', she picks herself up and tries again. Anna notices how they both like to be outside and how calm they are in the open. Beni likes to watch birds nearby on the feeder and Anna has arranged a number of household items around the garden over which Shari can safely climb. She often takes lunch outside and sings with the babies or shares a picture book.

Look, listen and note

Anna has worked hard to establish a good relationship with each of these babies. She offers both a lot of physical contact and comfort, allowing them to 'crawl all over her', and responds when they smile, vocalise or touch her. She imitates what they do and is pleased when they copy her. She notices that Beni is beginning to move his limbs with some intentionality. She recognises the impact each has on the other and provides opportunities for them to interact. Make sure your provision offers:

- sufficient time with the key worker to develop strong relationships, so that the adults know what the babies like and the babies can build up trust as they begin to move;

- space and opportunity for young babies to exercise their bodies, free from tight clothing or bedclothes – place them on the floor on a variety of different surfaces.

Effective practice

Anna is tuned in to each of these babies, knows what to expect at their phase of development and knows how to encourage the next steps. She offers stimulation and different opportunities for each to develop, using household objects as well as some commercial toys. She knows a range of nursery rhymes and has picture books to engage babies, developing their attention and listening skills. She plays 'Round and Round the Garden' or 'Peek-a-Boo' when the babies are little and graduates to movement rhymes such as 'Ring a Ring of Roses' as the children become more mobile. She understands how important it is to go outside as often as possible and provides a range of large motor activities out there for Shari who is engrossed in her new-found walking abilities. Anna joins in the childminders' group at the local children's centre, enjoying the exchange of ideas and the opportunity for Shari especially to play with other children and use the large climbing frames and other equipment. Ensure your setting provides:

- opportunities for when babies start to move – watch closely for that moment, following the baby's individual progress rather than a textbook timeline;

- times when toddlers can help – give them little jobs to do: ask them to bring an item for baby, to put something in the bin or to see if someone is coming.

Planning and resourcing

Anna is confident enough in her own knowledge to provide for what each baby is doing now and to offer an acceptable challenge to them when they are ready. She will construct a new piece of equipment when she sees it is needed or occasionally will buy something that will engage the babies' thinking. For example, she will make big picture books with different textures or sew a cushion for initial climbing purposes. She has recorded CDs with a variety of music for accompanying movement, such as dancing, or to calm the babies. In your setting:

- Rearrange the furniture and equipment so that babies and toddlers are supported as they start to move. Wherever possible, provide equipment that they can crawl through or walk over. Use large foam blocks or ball pools to provide experiences to exercise different muscles.

- Stimulate all the senses, not just sight and touch. Provide different smells and sounds, not just music. Record everyday sounds like traffic, trains and animal noises for toddlers to recognise as they grow. Encourage them to make their own noises and music.

Home links

Anna talks over with their parents what they are doing at home and ensures that routines match as closely as possible. She will take note of any new development the parents have seen and will extend this in her setting. Anna and the parents exchange photographs of significant events and often toys and other items too, so that there is continuity between what the parents do at home and what Anna offers. Does your setting offer:

- a joint record-keeping approach so that significant events can be logged and particular likes and dislikes noted?

- a chance for parents to talk through their practice at home, discussing their expectations and preferences, particularly if a child has an additional need?

Additional activities

- Hang wind chimes, mobiles made of translucent coloured materials which catch the sun outside to capture babies' attention.

- Move babies' bodies in time to music. Dance with them.

- As babies begin to sit more securely, provide 'treasure baskets' filled with everyday articles which are safe to handle and chew.

Change these frequently and theme them, e.g. items that make a noise, things that shine.

- As babies begin to crawl, motivate them to move by placing a toy just far enough away to present a challenge.
- As they begin to walk, provide a selection of wheeled toys that can offer them stable support.

From 16–26 months

Development matters

- Have a biological drive to use their bodies and develop their physical skills.
- Express themselves through action and sound.
- Are excited by their own increasing mobility and often set their own challenges.

Key words

tirelessness, challenge, excitement

From 22–36 months

Development matters

- Gradually gain control of their whole bodies and are becoming aware of how to negotiate the space and objects around them.
- Move spontaneously within available space.
- Respond to rhythm, music and story by means of gesture and movement.
- Are able to stop.
- Manage body to create intended movements.
- Combine and repeat a range of movements.

Key words

whole body control, spontaneous use of space, whole body response to stimulation, combination of movements

Scenario 2

The Magpie Nursery admits children between two and four years old. Although it has no safe outside area, it is spacious indoors and practitioners have created an area with soft flooring, foam blocks, cushions and shallow ramps for the toddlers and young children to use. Sometimes they hang soft hoops and spheres from the climbing frame for the toddlers to kick. Staff members notice that they become quite competitive in seeing who can kick these highest and challenge each other, squealing with delight. They have collected together a range of music and natural sounds, such as whale song, waterfalls and jungle noise. These encourage children to move rhythmically in time to them. As the children become confident, they are allowed to choose and put on the CDs for themselves. Practitioners join in and model what they can do. To counteract the lack of outside space, there are frequent trips to the nearby park. Here there are opportunities to swing and bounce on small wooden animals mounted on springs. The space offers chances for chasing and playing 'Follow my Leader' and 'Hide and Seek'. Both children and staff really like to play 'What's the Time, Mr Wolf?' and the children learn to stop very quickly. They notice how quickly the younger toddlers imitate the older ones and try to join in these games.

Look, listen and note

The team is committed to offering a good experience for physical development. Practitioners have built up a good supply of items which they swap around, making sure that there is sufficient to meet the needs of all the toddlers, providing challenges as they become more competent. They recognise that the toddlers like to imitate what they see adults do and play lots of movement games, such as 'Simon Says', which everyone enjoys. Make sure your setting offers:

- opportunities to observe what toddlers and young children do to build on pre-existing skills – turn everyday routines into times to experiment with new movements and vocabulary: bounce to the bathroom, glide to the garden, spin to the sunshine, rock in the reading corner and so on;

- examples for toddlers to imitate in beginning to move imaginatively, such as looking at how different dancers or animals move – join in with the children and ask them to guess what animal you are.

Effective practice

The team recognises the need to compensate for the lack of outside play space and it is rare not to go to the park during the session. The park not only provides space for the toddlers to run around and use the equipment; the journey also offers a chance to establish safety rules about using the roads. Inside, play space is available during the day for the children to keep active and explore and practise new movements, supported by a variety of sound, music and other stimuli. Does your setting offer:

- safe space set aside for the children to be energetic when they need to be, but also areas to rest and be quiet?

- recognition that many children develop schemas which capture particular interests?

How do you support and extend these?

Planning and resourcing

'Park time' is written into the nursery's routine and happens nearly every day. The team thinks seriously about what it offers individual children at each end of the spectrum of development and writes ideas into each child's plans. For example, they have a little girl with Down syndrome who needs plenty of practice with movement, and she is encouraged to join in 'rough and tumble' with a member of staff every day. Creating the movement corner (see p. 58) has proved inexpensive. The team has enjoyed being creative with what the group already owns, supplementing with items, such as ramps, which can be used for a variety of purposes. Ensure that your setting provides:

- a variety of equipment that can be used in different ways, like ramps, large cardboard boxes, large industrial tubing in a variety of colours, bricks and planks are a good start; inflatable items, like empty paddling pools, can turn into all sorts of props;

- opportunities for toddlers and young children to practise and experiment, making sure that the equipment and areas where they can do this freely are safe.

Explain the safety 'rules' to children and record these pictorially in ways children can understand and display.

Home links

Parents here share the record-keeping and add photos or anecdotes to their child's folder. There is an open invitation to join the group in the park, and many do this. Grandparents often come along too and it is good for the children to hear the childhood stories that relatives bring to these joint sessions. The easy relationship that parents and staff have reflects in the work of the nursery, and the children become more confident in knowing that aims are shared. Make sure you:

- ask parents and other relatives to plan and join in specific activities, such as dance, exercise, gardening and building;

- choose outings that families and children can share;

- keep a record in pictures, photos and writing of what happened during the visit that toddlers and young children can review and play out in the setting.

Additional activities

- Provide toddlers with a variety of different surfaces to walk and climb over, such as grass, mud, pebbles, ramps and small walls or benches.

- Introduce trikes and other wheeled toys, particularly those that can be used by more than one child.

- Ensure there is a variety of activities and items that develop fine motor control. Use everyday items wherever possible, e.g. real cutlery and crockery.

- Introduce simple stories and rhymes which they can act out physically. Use examples which involve groups of children and can be used repetitively.

- Use new vocabulary so that toddlers and young children learn new words and use them to describe what they are doing.

From 30–50 months

Development matters

- Move freely with pleasure and confidence in a range of ways, such as slithering, shuffling, rolling, crawling and walking, running, jumping, skipping, sliding and hopping.

- Use movement to express feelings.

- Negotiate space successfully when playing racing and chasing games with other children, adjusting speed or changing direction to avoid obstacles.

- Sit up, stand up and balance on various parts of the body.

- Demonstrate the control necessary to hold a shape or fixed position.

- Operate equipment by means of pushing and pulling movements.

- Mount stairs, steps or climbing equipment using alternate feet.

films as a source and provide dressing-up clothes that enhance their physical play;

- alert to space limitations and works with the children to make best use of what is available: small spaces can be used for contained, more complex, movements such as hopping like a rabbit, jumping like a frog or wriggling like a worm; *Follow My Leader*, for example, encourages children to think about their actions and consider others in their use of space.

Effective practice

Mandy is prepared to spend time and effort in expanding the children's imaginative movement, thinking creatively about ways to supplement what is available in the unit. There is never any hint of dismissing these ideas because they emanate from the TV. She values the children's choices. She takes her lead from the children and understands where each child is in his or her physical development as well as his or her thinking. She is prepared, for example, to allow the children to help her turn the TARDIS, as well as to man the interactive whiteboard, which needs exact fine motor control. She knows how to support those who are anxious to enter the TARDIS, and everyone does in the end. As an adult, she provides a good model to the children. She explores physical feelings, such as dizziness and anxiety, with each child and, together, they find reasons for it. Such results are never dismissed as 'making a fuss' – disorientation exists and is explored. Make sure your setting considers:

- how to encourage the more timid to attempt new activities: let them try things out with others – with an adult, in small peer groups, with a friend; let them sit and watch until they feel ready to join in; gently persuade, but never force;

- the variety of feelings that can be expressed through physical activity and the vocabulary that supports this: for example, space travel offers experiences to do with excitement, fear, weightlessness or speed and how to keep safe in unknown places.

Planning and resourcing

This early years unit is already planning in accordance with EYFS expectations. Mandy has considered the implications of this and understands the expectations of the physical-development strand. It is an area close to her heart and she has considered how she can implement its requirements in the situation she finds herself in. Space is a serious limitation, but, by linking this to movement and imagination, she can scaffold the children's learning by suggestions that expand their thinking. She is aware of each child's needs and makes copious, but significant, notes from her observations of each child for the records and to inform her as she plans next stages. These are integrated into each child's learning story and are always accompanied by photos taken throughout the day. Make sure your setting:

- records events and moments not only for assessment purposes but also for the children to recall, review and improve on previous occasions: for example, taking a video of a dance routine can help children see where they could add in something new or make movements more precise;

- offers opportunities to use a larger space each day, such as a park, school playground or hall; make sure that there is a supply of large equipment which is easy to move; let children help whenever possible, explaining the rules on safety and use of space.

Home links

This unit has a good rapport with parents. The first half hour each day allows for mothers and fathers to visit and spend time with their children, seeing what they have done and sharing ideas. Parents make suggestions and bring in items to augment play, such as items from the seashore. Make sure your setting encourages parents to:

- remember their childhoods and talk through with their children the things they enjoyed doing: invite them to share these with other children in your group; suggest they write the stories down or record them on tape;

- think of ways to involve their children in physical activities that do not stretch the family budget (see p. 59); helping at home with washing, safe DIY and cleaning offer opportunities as does using woods and parks for ball and chasing games.

Additional activities

- Make sure space is available for movement throughout the day so that children can choose when to use it. Use the movement corner idea, adding new items regularly.

- Introduce games and singing rhymes where there are rules or where accurate sequences of movement are required, such as 'The Hokey Cokey' or 'In and Out the Dusky Bluebells'. Old party games can take on a new lease of life: 'Blind Man's Bluff', 'Hunt the Thimble' or 'Musical Chairs' can all be adapted to different contexts.

- Provide challenging and changing climbing equipment. Ask the children to design it with you and consider safety rules for the group. These can be displayed in pictures and words near the equipment.

- Stories can be more complicated now. Help children make up their own and record them in photographs or by video which children can talk about and add extra ideas.

- Support children to build the props needed for their stories, such as the bridge in 'Three Billy Goats Gruff'.

Resources

Books which give general guidance in this aspect include:

- Quinn, J. and Wager, N. (2004) *The Little Book of Dance* (book and CD), Husbands Bosworth: Featherstone Education Ltd.

Roberts, A. and Featherstone, S. (2007) *The Little Book of Treasure Baskets,* Husbands Bosworth: Featherstone Education Ltd.

Babies and toddlers enjoy visual stimulation, music and different materials to touch and explore in their mouths. A good resource, whether it is made or bought, will cover a number of these aspects. A good example from birth is the following rag book, which is safe to chew, has black and white pictures of faces, crinkles when touched and has a mirror for the babies to see their own faces:

Fordham, J. (2002) *Faces* (Baby's Very First Book), London: Macmillan.

A number of books exist that will build up a range of finger and singing games. Everyone has his or her own favourites. These are some of mine:

Featherstone, S. and Williams, L. (2007) *Finger Play and Nursery Rhymes: Progression in Play for Babies and Children,* Husbands Bosworth: Featherstone Education.

Hindley, J. and Granstrom, B. (2000) *Eyes, Nose, Fingers and Toes,* London: Walker.

Sharratt, N. (2006) *Don't Put Your Finger in the Jelly, Nelly,* London: Scholastic.

Stoppard, M. (2007) *Baby Games,* London: Dorling Kindersley.

Good starting points for children to extend their movement repertoire are traditional rhymes and stories, such as 'Three Billy Goats Gruff' or 'The Three Little Pigs'. There are also modern classics, such as 'We're Going on a Bear Hunt', which are very good to initiate imaginative movement. Many of these tales are published in up-to-date editions and have taped stories and music which children can use themselves. These are easy to share with parents. A selection includes:

Berenstain, S. and Berenstain, J. (1991) *Bears in the Night,* Glasgow: HarperCollins.

Burningham, J. (2001) *Mr Gumpy's Outing,* London: Red Fox.

Hutchins, P. (2001) *Rosie's Walk,* London: Red Fox.

Prater, J. (1995) *You Can't Catch Me!* London: Red Fox.

Rosen, M. and Oxenbury, H. (1993) *We're Going on a Bear Hunt,* London: Walker.

Sendak, M. (2000) *Where the Wild Things Are,* London: Red Fox.

There are websites that will support you in this area; some provide free downloadable resources, such as http://www.yellowdoor.net. The Youth Sport Trust has just updated its early years programmes. Details can be found at http:/www.youthsporttrust.org.

Thinking about health and bodily awareness

Aims

By the end of this chapter, you should understand more fully what is involved in keeping healthy. This will reflect on mental as well as physical health and how we can be proactive in preventing ill-health. Being healthy includes well-being and consideration will be given to children's levels of stress and the impact that this can have on physical and mental health. The importance of adults as good role models in children's lives will be explored alongside ways to help children to take on responsibility for their own health and welfare as they grow older. The idea that many settings provide a haven of peace and safety for children in today's stressful society will be explored and its implications analysed. Your role in advising parents and carers will be considered. The following chapter gives guidance on implementing this aspect of the EYFS in your setting.

Introduction

This aspect of the EYFS addresses some of the tensions in the lives of children and families today and the contradictions in guidance and legislation which is meant to support them. As we consider elsewhere in this book, there has been conflict in how childhood and child development are understood in the UK, which has led to confusion in thinking how best to provide for children. This has occurred at a time when parents and others are under more stress themselves to perform at work and to maintain

What are friends for? (3 years 5 months)

particular lifestyles. Concerns about the level of relative poverty in the UK led in 1999 to the government campaign to eradicate childhood poverty by 2010. Facts about childhood poverty in the UK, one of the highest amongst industrialised nations, can be found on the End Child Poverty website (www.endchildpoverty.org.uk). Material poverty is accompanied by time poverty, where fewer and fewer adults spend time playing with their children. Alongside this, life is considered to be far more dangerous for young children, and this has had consequences in the way they are protected and prevented from experiencing some of the freedoms of earlier generations. Of course, work has had benefits as well, but the overall impression is that UK children in general do not experience a very good childhood in comparison to European counterparts.

In exploring this section of the EYFS, 'health' embraces not only physical but also mental health. It is taken to be proactive, rather than reactive, and considers some of the recent campaigns that support improvement in the way we maintain children's overall health. Angela Underdown (2006) has explored the factors in today's society which contribute to or detract from children's health and well-being, citing poverty, relative poverty and health inequalities, stress, the impact of family change on children's health and well-being, child public health and children's own involvement in health issues as some of the issues involved. Added to these is the infants' own growing sense of self-awareness, as individuals separate from their mothers or other intimate caretakers and become able to make decisions for themselves. Researchers have now worked out that babies have far more of a sense of self than previously thought (for example, see Rochat 2003). This has implications for the ways in which practitioners work with babies and infants, to see them as individuals in their world and to develop this sense of self. Scottish early years documentation recognises this: 'As they develop physically children also begin to become aware of themselves as individuals. This developing sense of identity is linked closely to their own self-image, self-esteem and confidence' (Scottish Consultative Council on the Curriculum 2001: Section 2: 36).

Good self-esteem is important to well-being, and many children are subject to negative environments even if this does not, in a formal sense, amount to a child-protection issue. Child-protection procedures depend on a description of the form of abuse experienced; physical and sexual abuse and neglect are usually apparent, although care must always be taken in interpreting what we see; emotional neglect may be far more pervasive and have long-lasting effects but is much harder to ascertain.

A good overview and discussion of the key issues in child health, as well as relevant readings, are provided by Silberfeld (2007: 49), who cautions:

> In marked contrast to the contemporary concept of the child as an individual and an understanding that child health and development in children cannot be predestined, the new EYFS offers guidance

about child health and development which is firmly rooted in an age-stage framework, which, however comprehensive, remains de-contextualised. This does not encourage the professional or practitioner to look at the child in its cultural, social, political and economic context.

Silberfeld is anxious that with little time and resources what a practitioner can achieve may be limited to what is on 'the checklist of requirements' (2007: 49). A real commitment to improving children's overall health will, therefore, involve all the practitioner's ingenuity and creativity.

Stress

One aspect that is increasingly worrying, however, affecting the mental health of the young, is the growing stress placed on children. This may result from family breakdown or from living in relative poverty or in situations which are not conducive to happy childhoods. Much of this stress can also be placed at the feet of governments who insist on early intervention and formal schooling not only to prevent later educational failure but also to instil skills to ensure that the UK remains at the top of the economic ladder. Mothers are expected to return to work, especially if they are single. Not only are children and young people the most highly tested in the world, but all kinds of educational provision, from the largest school to the smallest playgroup, have been subjected to vigorous inspection with results not only reflected in league tables but also undermining local communities' confidence in what they have to offer. This may not be purely 'academic' but may be far more in tune with health needs, both physical and mental; these are difficult to capture in an inspection that has predetermined areas for review. Contrast this with the situation in Swedish early years provision (Teachers' TV 2007). Children are also quick to pick up on adults' stress. They know when people important to them are under pressure and act accordingly. They absorb anxieties, and this can increase the levels of detrimental chemicals in the body's systems, particularly the brain (Gerhardt 2004).

In 2007, UNICEF's Innocenti Research Centre published *Child Poverty in Perspective: An Overview of Child Well-Being in Rich Countries*. This report placed the UK bottom or near bottom on all the parameters that the research measured. Only health and safety received a middling score.

Children's and young people's viewpoints were included in the way these statistics were compiled, as well as indicators from government data. It led to headlines in the press which raged about unhappy childhoods and resulted in a raised profile for the Children's Society's national *Good Childhood Inquiry* which had started in September 2006. The evidence from the enquiry into health has now been published. In the introduction, Professors Maughan and Scott indicated, 'Perhaps the greatest volume of responses related to an issue barely acknowledged by past generations: children's mental health [...] Young people themselves highlighted the importance of being free from stress, pressure and worry' (The Children's Society 2008).

If we know there is a problem, how can we sort it when we cannot remove the pressures families are under, particularly as the costs of living rise and we are threatened with recession? One way is to offer a haven for children, where each child is accepted and valued. This seems trite, but I have often seen children devastated by a throwaway remark, not intended to hurt but doing so nonetheless. We may have to rethink our response to comforting unhappy children physically, not turning them away because what we do may be misconstrued. In interpreting the EYFS, the needs of the child must come first, not the perceived needs of the UK economy in the future. International models show that introducing a formal structure (even if this is termed 'play-based') does not meet children's needs. It does not mean, by establishing a truly 'child-centred' approach, we will be allowing them to run riot. The majority of children will impose their own structure, giving us time to work with those who will not. This extract helps to underpin such a child-centred approach:

> Time, and how children and adults use it, is central to the Reggio philosophy. The rhythm and pace of the child is always given overriding importance [...] This means really having time for children's thoughts and ideas, and giving value to their work, their conversations and their feelings by slowing down to listen to them.
>
> (Learning and Teaching Scotland 2006: 21)

Healthy eating

There is much concern in the wealthier nations of the world about obesity, particularly in children, and part of the EYFS's mission is to introduce children at an early age to a balanced diet. In recent years, there have been campaigns to encourage people to eat five portions of fruit and vegetables a day and to cut down on excessive salt, sugar and fat. Celebrity chefs have led campaigns to improve school dinners, and there are grumblings about the contents of lunchboxes and how much power staff have to remove the worst excesses. As most parents and many practitioners recognise, you can pack the healthiest lunchbox in the country but children will feed it to the birds given half a chance. Why does the situation seem so poor in the UK? In a number of visits to nurseries elsewhere, I have witnessed children eating a full dinner with no reliance on 'junk' food. In early years provision in Sweden, for example, all food, including bread, was prepared from basic ingredients on the premises (Teachers' TV 2007). Watching the preparation for lunchtime in Reggio Emilia, I saw children working in the kitchen alongside the cooks to prepare the food. This happened every day. The kitchen was the hub of the pre-school, and its cooks were fully integrated members of the staff. Other children set tables with linen cloths, proper cutlery, china and glass. Staff also sat down to a cooked meal every day and offered good role models. Rather than a sandwich in the staff room or a yogurt by the computer, food and its rituals are seen to be important in passing on the country's culture and expectations. When I first started to work in France alongside French early years professionals, the two-hour midday lunch irked me. Yet I came to see its value in forming relationships and sharing viewpoints, sometimes arguing. If UK children no longer have these experiences on a daily basis at home, perhaps it should become a priority of the early years setting? It is not just the quality of the food that is in question but also the time to sit, eat and enjoy.

Children are helped to try new foods if they are enticed. Many primary schools are now following through with using school grounds to grow food, as well as sourcing the produce they use locally. Dorset Cereals sponsor the Edible Playgrounds Project. Show gardens grown by the Project and displayed at two major exhibitions in 2008 gained gold medals. Their website offers children and practitioners many ideas, not only on growing but also on cooking produce as well (www.edibleplaygrounds.co.uk). Children in the UK rarely starve, even if they fill their tummies with nutritionally questionable food. A friend's daughter survived on peas and chocolate for many years. There are many social, economic and cultural dimensions to providing food and families, even with all the good will in the world, may not have the money or the time to prepare nutritionally valuable meals. What can we do to supplement this? It is hard as a parent to see a child go without, or as a cook or budget-holder to see food wasted, but persistence and guile can usually work in the end, even if it means a child will eat just two or three new items to start with. Involving children in producing and preparing food can give them far more of an incentive to try things out. The other side of this is ensuring that children drink adequately during the day and that mealtimes are regular to ensure that energy levels are maintained. In the days before breakfast clubs were the norm, we raided the free milk that children then received in the nursery early in the morning and bought fruit, cheese and acceptable biscuits and crackers for the children as soon as they arrived in school.

Other considerations

Children with additional needs warrant extra care to ensure their well-being. *Every Disabled Child Matters* parallels *Every Child Matters* (www.edcm.org. uk). Hannah, who suffered with quite a severe, intermittent hearing loss, was overcome with joy the first time she was supplied with hearing aids. From being morose and grumpy, never quite tuned into what was happening around her, she blossomed into a much more socially integrated and happy child, more willing to meet others' expectations because she was far more aware of her environment. Improvements in listening, spoken language and understanding added to her sense of well-being. She was also more energetic and thus healthier. Anyone with a sensory or physical disability uses far more energy in coping with his or her world; the ability to stay attentive and on task in a complex situation is exhausting. Compare this to the stress an adult experiences when learning a new subject or when attempting to understand what is being said in an unfamiliar language, even when there are no sensory impairments. A substantial amount of research has been undertaken in energy expenditure for those with a variety of physical difficulties. For example, one project which compared walking in those with typical development with those with cerebral palsy resulted in data that demonstrated more than nine times more energy was required for those with the more severe problems (Johnston et al. 2004).

'Health' also encompasses other disabilities which cannot always be prevented, but sensitive practitioners can work to reduce the risk of a special need becoming a special educational need by ensuring, as in Kati's example (see p. 48), that children are supported to do as much as is possible for themselves. This not only aids their physical development but also their self-esteem; it encourages motivation and independence. For Hannah, the practitioners listened to Mum's worries and voiced their own, so that her mother was confident to approach her GP to insist on a hearing test. Helping to identify needs early in children's lives (*not* in their school life) and badgering until they are investigated, should be part of an ongoing commitment to children. Sir John Michael's (2008) independent enquiry, *Healthcare for All*, highlights how often those with learning disabilities and their carers are poorly treated by the health services, perhaps because of an undervaluing of their lives. This includes children.

Questions

- What do you do now that ensures you remain healthy? Do you provide a good role model for parents and children? How can you share what you consider to be vital activities for staying healthy with others within your setting?

- Children are intrigued by the way their bodies work. What are the sorts of questions children ask? How have you supported their exploration and learning when these opportunities have arisen?

- Children's well-being will be of paramount importance in your work as an early years practitioner. Discuss what you think this involves with colleagues. How do you deal with a situation where your views of what is best for a child do not match those of his or her parents?

- How does your setting work with parents and the community to ensure that health issues are taken into consideration and opportunities are available both in nursery and at home to protect and improve children's health and well-being? How do you take differences in culture and social and economic backgrounds into account?

References

Gerhardt, S. (2004) *Why Love Matters,* London: Routledge.

Johnston, M. E., Moore, S. E., Quinn, L. T. and Smith, B. T. (2004) 'Energy Cost of Walking in Children with Cerebral Palsy', *Developmental Medicine and Child Neurology* 46: 34–8.

Learning and Teaching Scotland (2006) *The Reggio Emilia Approach to Early Years Education*, 2nd edn, Glasgow: Learning and Teaching Scotland.

Michael, J. (2008) 'Independent Inquiry into Access to Healthcare for People with Learning Disabilities'. Available online at http://www.iahpld.org.uk/index.html (accessed 4 September 2008).

Rochat, P. (2003) 'Five Levels of Self-Awareness As They Unfold Early in Life', *Consciousness and Cognition*, 12: 717–31.

Scottish Consultative Council on the Curriculum (2001) *A Curriculum Framework for Children 3 to 5*, Dundee: Learning and Teaching Scotland.

Silberfeld, C. (2007) 'Developing as a Strong and Healthy Child?', in M. Wild and H. Mitchell (eds), *Early Childhood Studies: Reflective Reader*, Exeter: Learning Matters.

Teachers' TV (2007) *How Do They Do It in Sweden?* Birmingham: Television Junction.

Underdown, A. (2006) *Young Children's Health and Well-Being*, Maidenhead: Open University Press.

7 Health and bodily awareness in practice

 The EYFS principles

Health and bodily awareness is about how children learn the importance of keeping healthy and the factors that contribute to maintaining their health (DfES 2007c).

- Physical development helps children to develop a positive sense of well-being.
- Physical development enables children to feel the positive benefits of being healthy and active.
- Physical development helps children gain confidence in what they can do.

Good health in the early years helps to safeguard health and well-being throughout life. It is important that children develop healthy habits when they first learn about food and activity. Growing with appropriate weight gain in the first years of life helps to guard against obesity in later life.

- Provide time to support children's understanding of how exercise, eating, sleeping and hygiene promote good health.
- Treat mealtimes as an opportunity to promote children's social development, while enjoying food and highlighting the importance of making healthy choices.

The EYFS offers developmental points for each age phase. Scenarios provide ideas in context and additional activities are suggested below. Resources to support the practitioner or the family are included at the end of this chapter. The information here should be cross-referenced to the practical guidance offered by the EYFS documentation. The NHS (2007) also provides detailed guidance in its publication *Birth to Five*.

From birth–11 months

Development matters

- Thrive when their nutritional needs are met.
- Respond to and thrive on warm, sensitive physical contact and care.

Key words

reciprocal relationships, contact, comfort, feeding, sleeping

From 8–20 months

Development matters

- Need rest and sleep, as well as food.
- Focus on what they want as they begin to crawl, pull to stand, creep, shuffle, walk or climb.

Key words

motivation, space, rest, positive support

From 16–26 months

Development matters

- Show some awareness of bladder and bowel urges.

- Develop their own likes and dislikes in food, drink and activity.

- Practise and develop what they can do.

Key words

choice, independence, exploration, practice, control

Let's go down to the woods today (Family outing)

Scenario 4

Anna enjoys mealtimes with the babies she cares for. Beni is still drinking milk from a bottle and has not yet started to try solids. This follows the advice given by the NHS and concurs with his mother's wishes. She is trying to maintain breastfeeding when she is able and supplies Anna with the bottles she requires. Anna ensures that there is always a quiet time for feeding as she thinks it is important for Beni to be calm, to have these moments for physical contact and to establish a rapport. She notices how he makes close eye contact and snuggles close to her. Anna makes sure he is clean and dry before he has his nap. Changing times are important for reciprocal 'chats': she always talks to him or sings, and he responds well. He has started to have little 'conversations' with her and mum has remarked on this too.

Shari is learning to be independent now and sometimes uses a beaker without its feeding top. She makes a mess, but Anna enjoys seeing the effort she puts into having a go and praises her achievements. Shari is starting to make choices about what she likes to eat. Her family is vegetarian and Anna makes certain that what she offers Shari matches her home diet. As her own daughter, Jojo, has an egg allergy, she is used to being careful and reading the small print on labels. Shari has started to use a spoon: though finger foods are still easier to manage, she wants to be independent and resists any attempts Anna makes to feed her. Shari's mum is relaxed about potty training, and, together, they have decided to leave it until Shari indicates herself that she is ready. Anna left Jojo until she was ready. Jojo wanted to go to the playgroup with her friends and needed to be clean and dry before she could. It took just a fortnight for her to be successful at just two and a half, both night and day. She needs help with her clothing but has had few accidents and so is very proud of herself. Both Shari and Jojo still need naps during the afternoon. Rather that struggle with either of them, Anna has created a cosy corner where they can both go for a nap if they are reluctant to settle into their beds. Both toddlers snuggle up with Anna on the sofa to rest, and sometimes they will have a little nap there. It is important for them to rest, both to replace the energy they expend but also so that they are not grumpy when with their parents in the evening.

Look, listen and note

Anna has established a basic routine but is flexible enough to meet all the children's needs. She has a relaxed manner, and the babies respond to this. She praises their achievements and is not critical of mess nor does she thwart their independence. Because of her qualities, neither baby is stressed and they are happy in her company and with each other. In your own setting ensure that:

- the key person concept moves beyond record-keeping to forming attachments to babies and toddlers so that they are secure and happy;

- practitioners can recognise the signs that indicate when babies are hungry, tired or need changing and respond quickly; this establishes trust and helps babies to learn how to exercise control in their environment.

Effective practice

Anna understands the babies and is very patient and kind towards them. She takes every opportunity, such as changing time, to talk and sing with them so that it is a pleasant experience. She exercises their limbs and plays games such as 'This Little Piggy'. She is pleased that Shari wants to be independent and accepts that part of this at the toddler phase is practising and making a mess. She uses her experience with Jojo as a guide but recognises all toddlers are different and will watch carefully for indications that Shari is ready to use the potty. Ensure in your own setting that:

- you offer opportunities for babies and toddlers to become independent as soon as they show signs they are ready: let babies hold their bottle (supervised) and toddlers dress and feed themselves, helping when they indicate; keep a good supply of dressing up clothes that are easy for toddlers to use (hats, cloaks fastened with Velcro, boots, etc.); let them help you;

- you are able to offer foods with different textures and consistencies so that babies and toddlers expand their likes and dislikes as well as practising feeding themselves; keep a note of what is liked or disliked and try to reintroduce things a little later.

Planning and resourcing

As far as possible, Anna follows the routines parents have established to help the babies feel comfortable and secure. She has gathered a good set of attractive resources, renewing them as soon as there are signs of wear and tear. She feels this is particularly important for feeding, changing and potty training. She has picture books she has gathered over the years but is always on the lookout for new titles. She especially likes those that the babies can look at themselves as soon as they are able and often uses them at quiet times when the babies need to rest but are not sleepy. She understands items will get battered and chewed but accepts this as part of their learning. In your setting, ensure that you always:

- provide a comfort corner where babies, toddlers and young children can choose to rest when they want and need to do so; ensure that there are toys to chew or cuddle and books to explore in this area;

- offer choice to babies and toddlers as soon as they are able to do this for food, drink and toileting requirements.

Home links

Anna has established with Beni and Shari's parents what they would like her to do regarding feeding and toilet-training. She respects their wishes and offers a plan of the week's menus to Shari's parents, though they accept that this may change. They trust that she will follow their dietary preferences closely. Anna takes digital photos to share with the families, and there is often laughter about the mess Shari creates. In this way, Shari meets the same positive reactions at home as she learns to feed herself. In your setting, ensure that:

- parents' wishes are respected and particular requests or cultural practices are followed through;

- there is always a moment to talk to a parent, even if it sometimes means making a phone call – make sure you share the good as well as the problematic moments.

Additional activities

- Babies and toddlers have different needs when it comes to sleep. Some sleep through the night very quickly but are awake and alert all day. Ensure their key worker is involved with them when they are awake and that they have objects to see, handle and mouth. Baby books made from different materials are good here; some have mirrors and make a variety of sounds.

- Build a bird table outside the window of the babies' room, so that they can watch and hear the birds (and sometimes see squirrels too). As they grow older, talk to the toddlers about the food and drink that birds like. Experiment!

- Some babies suffer when teething. Make sure they are comforted physically when in pain and irritable. Find objects for them to bite and chew if they are old enough: pieces of fruit and vegetables, such as carrot sticks and hard apple or pear pieces are good for this.

- All babies and toddlers enjoy playing with water. Let them do this as often as possible. Blow bubbles to capture babies' attention – toddlers will chase them as well.

- Eat with the children to provide a good role model and opportunities for conversation. Make sure it is relaxed and enjoyable for all. Celebrate special events with special mealtimes.

From 22–36 months

Development matters

- Communicate their needs for things such as food, drinks and when they are uncomfortable.

- Show emerging autonomy in self-care.

Key words

self-awareness, self-help, purposeful, interactive, curious

Scenario 5

Theo is just three and has been at the nursery school since the beginning of term. He is learning English as an additional language but there are no other speakers of his home language in the school. His grandmother spends the first fortnight with him, gradually withdrawing as he seems to settle. He has spent a lot of time watching the children from the sidelines and has just made his first attempts to join the activities on offer. He is quiet and prefers to stay alongside the nursery nurse with whom he has started to make an attachment.

Although tabletop and floor activities indoors are safe for him, as he settles he begins to look wistfully towards the garden. Children in this nursery school have open access to the outside area all day, whatever the weather, and boys in particular like to be outside. Eventually, Theo makes it outside. He appears fascinated by the slide and indicates through eye-pointing that he wishes to climb it. He does not want to hold hands with his nursery nurse. Although embedded in a soft, grassed bank, the slide is quite high and normally the preserve of older children. The nursery nurse has a dilemma. This is the first time that Theo has taken the lead in communicating with her and she does not want to lose his trust. She is unable to ask him, because of the language barriers, if he has done this before, nor, because of the immediacy of the moment, can she wait to contact his parents or grandmother (though there are language barriers there too). She makes a decision. Through gesture, drawing and by using another child as a model, she communicates with Theo that he can go up the slide but must hold her hand for the first three turns (at least) until they are both sure he can do it by himself. Theo nods in agreement, and off he goes. He is able to walk up the stairs step by step and position himself securely at the top to slide down. After a few attempts, the nursery nurse is happy to let him do this by himself, and he spends the next few days practising and gaining mastery of the slide, trying new ways of sliding down (see p. 33). Other children see this, and, by the end of the week, he has created a small friendship group centred on his prowess with the slide. A home visit is planned to learn more about Theo in his family context.

Look, listen and note

This example illustrates how all the child's development areas are interlinked. Through his success with the slide, Theo's social network is increased and his emotional security is enhanced. Physically, he is progressing well. He is secure in controlling his body to plan, organise and coordinate the movements necessary to use the slide effectively and, after a period of consolidation, to experiment with new series of movements. He is able to transfer this learning to other equipment such as the climbing frame and is able to ask for support when he recognises he needs it. His English has improved, and the team says his understanding is very good though he is shy of speaking. In your setting ensure that you:

- recognise what children are communicating to you, whatever means they use; this is particularly important when you do not share a spoken language so that safety issues are addressed but challenge is maintained;

- help young children to succeed in difficult physical manoeuvres as this improves their self-esteem as well as their physical development; offer a challenge that they can manage and allow time for practice so they gain mastery – you may be bored with the repetition, but they won't be.

Effective practice

This incident forms the basis of a group discussion on how to help Theo in nursery. The team recognises the need to focus on Theo and his family to ensure that they receive the support necessary for him to make the best of his time here. The team resolves to update its mission statement to reflect its intention to prepare more fully for children with an additional language. Although home visiting is not part of what this nursery usually offers, after seeing Theo at home, the team can see the benefits of it and aim to explore it when the nursery policies are next reviewed. Through the practitioners' sensitive and positive handling of the situation, Theo's well-being is assured, and he develops a good sense of identity. Ensure that your setting provides:

- not just a paper policy but also a deep commitment to and understanding of children and families who are new to the country or area or have suffered traumatic events in their lives: collect information for families in the form of books, pamphlets and websites which are easily accessible; wherever possible, make sure these are available in a range of relevant languages – try to learn a few words yourself;

- resources for children that not only reflect different ethnic and cultural groups but also help with the idea of change or moving from one society to another – children's videos can sometimes help: the classic *The Snowman* helps with change and loss of a friend, and I can remember an episode of *Rugrats* that dealt with moving to a new house.

Planning and resourcing

By reflecting what they have learnt from observing Theo in nursery then talking with his parents, his team is able to plan activities specifically for him, using his physical prowess as central to his social, emotional and language development. Activities are selected for outside which involve digging, planting and building frames to support the growing plants. This supports what Theo has seen in his home country before he moved to the UK and also his family's current interests. In this, Theo can take a lead and his father has also offered to come to nursery to help the staff with this. Because of Theo's interests, a small trampoline is ordered for the nursery, which can be part-buried in the grassed area to keep it safe. Plans are made for more cooperative games, using balls and parachutes. Through these activities, Theo's confidence in his growing language skills becomes apparent, bilingual lists are created, and Theo becomes central in teaching staff and children words in his own language. In your setting, check if you fully consider:

- a child who has a particular preference, interest or talent and whether you encourage this – a visit to a Chinese or Italian restaurant could provoke a project which involves visits, cooking with family members, tasting new foods and reorganising the home corner into a restaurant or particular family home;

- children with additional languages are well supported and can be proud of their languages and use them.

Do not consider that learning another language is a 'problem'. Most people in the world speak at least two. This is also especially important if the additional language is sign. Teaching staff and children to sign ensures that the children (and often their families) are included in the life of the nursery.

Home links

The practitioners regret they did not anticipate Theo's entry to nursery fully and had not prepared themselves by learning a few essential words of the family language, engaging more with his parents to do this, to find out relevant aspects of their history and of their culture. In planning the next steps for Theo, they arrange a home visit to see his parents in the evening. The effect of seeing his teacher and nursery nurse in his home setting is a positive one for Theo, and he is able to show them his favourite toys and photos of activities he enjoys. The adults explore together what the expectations are for Theo in nursery and where to go next. It is established that Theo loves to move and be physically active and goes to trampolining sessions each week, and the team supports this in nursery. Think about practice in your setting:

- Do you prepare fully for children's admission to the setting, learning about their family, interests and needs?

- Is the information you have 'active' or does it sit in the record folder?

- How sensitive are you to individual children's needs and experiences and how do you help them to settle?

Invite family or community members into the setting to sing or recite rhymes, to cook with the children or to demonstrate specific skills, such as embroidery or using chopsticks. At this age, children are proud when this happens and it reinforces well-being and sense of identity.

Additional activities

- Encourage children to talk about themselves and their family history. Make picture books with them and invite relatives in to talk to the children and tell stories. This leads to a positive sense of self.

- Offer choices in food and drink. Let the children help to serve others. Introduce new foods for them to try, particularly unusual ones. Link these to what you have learnt about cultural differences and preferences when talking with families.

- Talk to the children about their need to be comfortable, clean and dry. Use picture books, which are straightforward and sometimes funny.

- Ensure home corners and play equipment offer real objects and opportunities for health and hygiene to become part of their play, for example, things for preparing a snack. Investigate the Montessori approach to this.

- Make sure that bathrooms are nice and bright, with pictures and plants, so that toddlers and young children like to use them.

From 30–50 months

Development matters

- Show awareness of own needs with regard to eating, sleeping and hygiene.

- Often need adult support to meet those needs.

- Show awareness of a range of healthy practices with regard to eating, sleeping and hygiene.

- Observe the effects of activity on their bodies.

Key words

collaboration, questioning, self-care

From 40–60+ months

Development matters

- Show some understanding that good practices with regard to exercise, eating, sleeping and hygiene can contribute to good health.

Key words

mastery, understanding, independence

Scenario 6

Mina was pleased with her project on integrating the senses (see p. 34). She had noted during this how children were willing to taste new foods in their play with feely boxes, even when they were reluctant to do so in more formal snack times and at lunch. She had read about Reggio Emilia and other countries in mainland Europe where the kitchen formed the hub of the nursery and wished to experiment more with growing and preparing food in the UK. She wanted to involve all the children who attended, between the ages of 2 and 5 years, to make nutrition an essential, central and enjoyable part of the children's lives, rather than the battleground it often became. Rather than just asking parents to provide fruit and other interesting food items, she wanted children to be immersed in the whole cycle of food growth, production and preparation, believing this was the way to ensure children's interest and understanding. She had been horrified to realise that children saw no connection between a chip or crisp and a potato and set about to change this, long before celebrity chefs had a hand in school meals. She found that, by extending the feely box idea, she was initially able to introduce children to new tastes as part of their play. Children were invited to bring in foodstuffs, and they gained a sense of pride when others liked their choice. Eventually she was able to create a vegetable and fruit garden in the grounds of the school which the whole community supported and protected. Through this, not only did she achieve her aim, but children and families also improved their knowledge and practical ability to provide nutritionally balanced meals. An offshoot of this was a sensory garden where herbs and other strongly smelling plants, plants with different textures and others with bright colours were cultivated for a child with impaired vision and her family.

Look, listen and note

Mina used a play situation to bring about change in children's willingness to try new foods and so to improve their diets. She saw that the community was struggling with healthy eating and was ready to accept some help, but she remained aware that not everyone could afford to buy more expensive fruit and vegetables. Through the practical activities she introduced, Mina was able to highlight hygiene and safety aspects, especially when cooking where cleanliness and using tools sensibly were essential.

- Link what the children are doing with the needs of the wider community. Cooking and growing food is an obvious choice, but children's centres offer a range of other activities, such as exercise and dance. Organising joint activities like sponsored races, trike rides or obstacle courses is enjoyable, healthy, brings the nursery and community together and can raise money for specific items or projects.

- Develop children's fine motor skills through practical activities which are useful, in context and reinforce hygiene aspects. Small children love to help out in the 'real world', using a brush and dustpan, washing a small item of clothing or preparing a real snack with proper cutlery and crockery, then washing up. Through these, concepts of safety (using a knife carefully) and hygiene (washing yourself and personal items) can be instilled.

Effective practice

Starting from the original game Mina was able, with the parents' support, to build on it and develop new ideas and activities. She recognised that developing the garden offered opportunities for all children to be involved, to develop safe working practices and to help children monitor the effects of exercise on their bodies. They also began to understand life cycles and the need for patience. In your setting:

- Ensure there are opportunities for children to exercise sufficiently so that their heart rates increase and they become hot and sweaty.

- Invite them to explain this to you and discuss how the body reacts when this happens and what they need to do to return to normality.

- Show them how to take their pulse and how to compare heart rates when resting, during everyday activities and after exercising. Produce charts.

Planning and resourcing

This project had to be planned carefully and in small steps, taking into account not only the needs of the children but also those of the staff and local community. Mina was able to counter the negativity she first met towards this project ('My child will never eat that!') through her observations of what children were doing in their play. She built on an interest already there. Careful planning proved valuable in ensuring that skills were developed and that understanding about nutrition and the way the body works was embedded. Practical resources at first were available from the nursery budget and with the help of the families (utensils, food stuffs, seeds) but later supplemented by donations of materials sought from various places through fundraising and charitable donations. In your setting:

- Ensure that projects link to children's interests and that you have sufficient resources to sustain and expand them so that children can see things through from beginning to end. They need to have a good deal of control and choice over what happens. In one nursery, a child's passion for the body and learning how it works led to a project that involved all the children. The starting point for this was a skeleton that practitioners borrowed from the local hospital. Projects from Reggio Emilia have included the local sewer network, angels, birth and building a birdtable.

- Ensure that your planning includes all the children, like the sensory garden above. Raised beds allow children in wheelchairs to join in, and those with significant learning difficulties can enjoy what the outside has to offer: flowers, birds, clouds, trees.

Home links

Understanding her community, Mina was able to form a strong partnership with it, allowing everyone to work together to make this a success. As the families felt they owned the project and were benefiting from it, they were willing to give their time to practical help and administration. Much of the help she received came from fathers and grandparents, willing to give their time to developing the garden and working alongside the children. She uncovered a number of skills which her families had not revealed to the nursery, such as bakery, which she used to good effect. She was also able to include a family, all of whom had varying degrees of impaired vision, both into the school and their community. In your setting:

- Ensure that parents are not just informed but share their children's care and education. This can happen through daily contact, home visits, frequent photos, open days and workshops, as well as being part of the ongoing project described above. Parents and other family members have a lot to offer, and establishing good relations at this age helps to ensure that they stay involved positively as children become older. Children gain a better sense of well-being and stress is reduced if setting and family work together well.

Additional activities

- Ask a mother to bring in her baby and bathe him or her in the group. Talk about a baby's needs and how these are met.

- Talk about and record what happens to the children's bodies when they are very cold, very hot or after exercise.

- Bring in visitors to talk about caring for themselves, like the school nurse, dentist or ophthalmologist.

- Make visits to local facilities such as the fruit and vegetable market, health clinic and sports club.

- Initiate a project on sleep. Make picture stories, charts and graphs.

Resources

The Department of Health's *Healthy Schools Programme* is now extending to pre-schools. Details, including case studies, can be found at: http://www.healthyschools.gov.uk/Beyond-Early-Years.aspx

Stories are always a good starting point for interesting children in a new project. Traditional fairy stories, like 'The Enormous Turnip', 'Goldilocks and the Three Bears' or 'Jack and the Beanstalk', are relevant and also provide stimuli for acting out and using movement in children's play.

They will also introduce information about the body and the concept of growth into your discussions with toddlers and children and will explore some feelings, too. Many are classics which are reprinted time and again. This indicates that they are loved by children! Great numbers of board books exist for use with babies and toddlers, starting from photos of real objects and moving on to drawings and paintings. Many of these will not have words, and it is good to make up your own dialogue, based on what you have shared together. Good storybooks are also available in different languages or dual languages. You will have your own favourite books, but these are some which I have enjoyed with children:

Food and eating

Browne, E. (1995) *Handa's Surprise,* London: Walker Books. (A good one to act out.)

Child, L. (2003) *I Will Never Not Ever Eat a Tomato,* Cambridge, Mass.: Candlewick Press.

Cooper, H. (2005) *A Pipkin of Pepper,* London: Corgi Children's Books.

Cooper, H. (2007) *Pumpkin Soup,* London: Corgi Children's Books.

Cooper, H. (2007) *Delicious!* London: Children's Books.

Pelham, D. (1990) *Sam's Sandwich,* London: Jonathon Cape. (Not for the squeamish but good fun! A book for individuals or small groups.)

Ross, T. (2008) *I Don't Like Salad!* London: Andersen.

The body, growth and change

Ahlberg, A. and Ahlberg, J. (1999) *Funnybones,* London: Puffin. (The start of a series.)

Baker, J. (2002) *Window,* London: Walker Books.

Baker, J. (2004) *Belonging,* London: Walker Books.

Carle, E. (1999) *From Head to Toe,* London: Puffin.

Carle, E. (2002) *The Very Hungry Caterpillar,* London: Puffin.

Cooper, H. (1997) *The Baby Who Wouldn't Go to Sleep,* London: Corgi Children's Books.

Hutchins, P. (1991) *Titch,* London: Jonathon Cape.

Willis, J. and Millward, G. (2008) *The Bog Baby,* London: Puffin.

Hygiene

Light, J. and Evans, L. (2006) *The Flower,* Swindon: Child's Play. (An interesting book about a city with no flowers; best read with older children in small groups with an adult who can draw out questions sensitively.)

Muller, G. (1989) *Garden in the City,* Macdonald.

Petty, K. and Maizels, J. (2005) *The Global Garden,* London: Random House. (A special pop-up book, based on the Eden Project in Cornwall.)

Prater, J. (1995) *You Can't Catch Me!* London: Red Fox.

Ross, T. (2000) *I Want My Potty!* London: Andersen Gardens.

Von Olfers, S. (2007) *Mother Earth and her Children,* updated by S. Schoen Smith, Elmhurst, Ill.: Breckling Press.

Feelings

Gravett, E. (2007) *Little Mouse's Big Book of Fears,* Basingstoke: Macmillan. (A nice book about facing different anxieties when you are little with an interesting twist at the end.)

Tan, S. (2001) *The Red Tree,* Sydney: Lothian. (This book should be used with an adult as it deals with depression in children.)

Shaun Tan has also written *The Arrival* (2006, publisher as above). This is much more for adults but could be used with parents who have moved from other communities in the world to establish a common understanding of immigration.

Many classic children's stories are accompanied by CDs so that children can listen again to the stories. Some now have been filmed, but you will need to use your own judgement in deciding whether it is good practice to show videos in your setting.

Many recipe books exist for children and parents to use. These are two books to do with food and cooking that I particularly enjoy:

- Buller, L. (2005) *Food,* London: Dorling Kindersley.

- Wilkes, A. and Watt, F. (2000) *The Usborne Children's World Cookbook,* London: Usborne Publishing.

There are a number of practical books which have been published over the years which are aimed at children and gardens. These include some classics as well as more recent publications:

- Dorling Kindersley (2008) *Grow It, Eat It,* London: Dorling Kindersley.

- Featherstone, S. (2003) *The Little Book of Growing Things,* Husbands Bosworth: Featherstone Education.

- Krezel, C. and Curtis, B. (2006) *Kids Container Gardening,* Batavia, Ill.: Ball Publishing.

- Murphy, D. (2008) *The Playground Potting Shed,* London: Guardian Books.

- Wilde, K. (2005) *Gardening with Children,* London: Collins.

A number of websites now exist which can support groups interested in developing their outside areas into productive gardens. These are of interest not only to practitioners and families but also to older children. For example:

- Dorset Cereals (undated) Edible Playgrounds Project: www.edible playgrounds.co.uk

- Royal Horticultural Society (RHS)/Campaign for School Gardening: www.rhs.org.uk/schoolgardening

As well as from educational suppliers, reasonably priced equipment for cooking or gardening can be found by surfing the Internet. The Amazon.

co.uk site provides a number of links as well as supplying books at good prices. Additional guidance is circulated to all new parents via:

📖 NHS (2007) *Birth to Five,* London: Department of Health. Available online at http://www.dh.gov.uk/en/Publicationsandstatistics/Publications/PublicationsPolicyAndGuidance/DH_074924.

8 Thinking about using equipment and materials

Aims

By the end of this chapter you should be able to audit your provision with respect to physical development to ensure that all you have is used fully and to identify gaps which need to be filled. You will have a greater understanding of the role of toys and playthings in young children's lives and how simple items can provide good physical and imaginative experiences. Gaps may include the need to look for community resources beyond your setting or training issues, where development plans are needed to ensure that staff members are fully conversant with this area of development, resource management or health and safety issues. Design issues are considered. The following chapter offers advice on putting this strand of the EYFS into practice.

Introduction

We believe that play environments should be beautiful, individually designed, should please and stimulate the senses, and be sources of delight and surprise. Nothing less will do.

(Free Play Network/Playlink exhibition,
Places of Woe: Places of Possibility)

I'm going to be a star! (5 months)

This chapter extends the thinking in this section of the EYFS to include not only equipment but also the use of the outside and the human resources needed to ensure whatever the setting possesses is used to its full potential.

While I was researching and writing this book, I had a dream which I remembered vividly. I do not have many I can recall; when I do, they are usually important. In this, I had just started to work in a nursery, for some reason quite a long way from my home. The day nursery offered full day care to babies and infants but only three appeared to be present that day. There was just one other member of staff. I remembered the accommodation clearly. The nursery was an old prefabricated building and comprised just two very large rooms, which were carpeted but almost bare. I had no sense that a kitchen, bathroom or small office were present. Storage was limited, and a few closed cupboards were along the walls, nothing at child height where playthings could be selected by the children. Windows, as they are in such buildings, were high up on the walls so that the children could not see out. The nursery seemed to be in a dip, approached by a steep ramp across grassed banks, unsuitable for toddler play. At the back was a shared, enclosed, grassed area, but the other practitioner said it was being used for sports day by the neighbouring school so we could not go out. The equipment in the nursery was disorganised. At the end of the day, I attempted to change the baby (for the first time?) on the floor in front of his mother and could not find half the items I needed. What had the children done all day? I had no sense that they were unhappy though the baby slept for most of the time the dream lasted – I made the excuse to his mum that he might be sickening for something, but, really, I think he was just bored to sleep. I cannot pinpoint what the other two were doing, but there was no attempt by the two adults to involve themselves in their play and to expand their knowledge and understanding of the world. The adults were quite happy to stand aside and talk 'adult' talk, not centred at all on the children. My co-worker was much more interested in how I was going to manage the journey to work every day.

The content of this dream surprised me. I had not been anywhere quite like this, so desolate in what it offered children, yet as I thought it through I could pinpoint very easily where I had had professional and personal experiences that matched those in the dream. I have been privileged to visit and work with hundreds of different kinds of early years provision throughout my career, and this scenario was an amalgamation of the worst practices I had seen, though never all in one place at any one time. Through the dream, the importance of good use of accommodation, resources and equipment was highlighted but the role of the practitioner was paramount. Why is it that some people manage to create an amazing environment for small children with very little in the way of material resources, yet others have beautiful accommodation and have spent much on materials but what they offer the children is sterile and devoid of feeling?

Leading from the children

Good early years practice always advocates starting from the child's interests. It is not always possible to provide what every child needs in a large early years unit, but listening to children will enable practitioners to think creatively in fulfilling individual needs as well as they can. This is integral to the philosophy behind Reggio Emilia's approach where adults support and extend children's ideas, enabling them to select their own themes and to devise and complete projects. Reggio Emilia centres are beautiful, but they are not full of boxes of brightly coloured, plastic equipment nor loads of electronic toys and gadgets. Good-quality materials for arts projects and activities are in abundance; otherwise, excellent use is made of found materials and objects, such as the coloured glass bottles, broken into small pieces to make the mosaics seen in each nursery. Collections of small natural items, like leaves, are used with light boxes and pieces of string, cotton and wools become complicated structures which hang in the breeze. Children see the possibilities of creating something new out of these objects, following the examples set by the adults who work with them. In one nursery, the staff had created beautiful flowers from used plastic bottles; the daylight shone through these, producing delicately coloured shadows on the white walls. Every item the children (or adults) produce is valued and displayed well at a height that children can see and easily handle.

Children often show a passionate interest in different aspects of physical play, and we need to support these with any activities and resources we can provide. Sometimes these early activities turn into a life-long interest, but not always. For Billy, balls always held a fascination. His ever-expanding collection included footballs, rugby balls, big balls, little balls, hard balls, soft balls, balls constructed of rubber bands and so on. Each of these varied in texture, sound and weight as well as size and offered a different physical and sensory experience. At just two he was videoed kicking a ball; he was accurate, and his balance was superb. Now much older, he plays football and rugby with much prowess, and his self-esteem and social world are very much connected to these activities. His family now admit it was worth living alongside early morning ball practice in their house to see the satisfaction he derives from this. This may represent a schema, in Athey's terms: 'A schema is a pattern of repeated actions. Clusters of schemas develop into later concepts' (2007: 115; see p. 31).

Small equipment

Taking into account the provisos above, each setting will prioritise its acquisition of small equipment and consumables. Pat Gura (1996) has used the term 'stuff' to cover all the materials found in a setting, whatever their origin. She rejects the description 'play material' deliberately as 'overworked and misleading'. Her reasons for doing this are clearly stated:

> Early learning makes use of stuff in both play and work contexts. Arguably, there is no material, or substance, not even a toy which is by its nature a play material. Anything can *become* a play material, as the player wills it: a child's duffle-coat worn by its owner as a Batman cape is a play material *while play lasts.*
>
> (1996: 1, italics in original)

John and Elizabeth Newson (1979: 255) concluded their classic study with, 'Some children would prefer an object which has never seen the inside of a toyshop at all. Perhaps in choosing a toy we need to shift our focus: to ask not "which toy?" but "what would this child enjoy doing, and what will meet that end?"'.

Infants will substitute one item for another as soon as they reach the point somewhere in the first year of their lives of moving on from real objects to toy representations. A small shoe will symbolise a cup, or a spoon will stand for a phone. Tovey points out how children transform their playthings and environments:

> Transformations include using one object, place or gesture to stand for another. For example, children might use a traffic cone to stand for a witch's hat or a ladder for a lawn mower or they transform a space in the bushes into a den or a climbing frame into a castle.
>
> (Tovey 2007: 19–20)

These transformations aid children's thinking and evidence the overlap between physical play and cognition. Good toys, or stuff, are 'good' because they are multipurpose; a good toy can become whatever it needs to be for the child over long periods of time. Examples pertinent to physical play include blocks and bricks, climbing frames and tools for digging. These do not come with a predestined purpose but depend on the child's creativity and imagination. 'Found' objects can have a just as important role; cardboard boxes can become houses, boats or a TARDIS (see p. 76), while many a small child has delighted in collections of stones and shells. In primary school, a friend and I played for two years, oblivious to those around us, creating a whole world out of small found objects in the playground: stones, twigs, sweet wrappers, leaves and petals. These small objects, delicate to handle and manipulate, were more precious and cared for even than the dolls and other commercial toys each of us had at home. Goldschmied has developed over many years the 'treasure basket' approach to babies' play, filling containers with everyday objects that intrigue babies and inviting them to explore each through their senses. Babies will start to play together, sharing a basket. Some commercial products can be replaced by stuff made by practitioners and children. Play dough is a good example of this. Playing with dough came second in one survey of children's favourite playthings (outside play was the first choice). Commercial play dough is relatively expensive and can be short-lived, succumbing to grubbiness and drying out. The recipe for making your own is freely available and lends itself to additional ingredients (see Appendix 2). Dough not only is calming, but using it promotes fine motor control and use of the senses. I have added strong perfumes to it (though children cannot then eat it) or natural flavourings such as vanilla and peppermint to support children with visual impairment. I have, on occasion, made it with wholemeal flour and added yellow food colouring – you can imagine the effect, but it fitted in well with talking about babies and the body. One child with Down syndrome I used to visit was causing some anxiety at his play group. He loved play dough but was inclined to eat it. The practitioners were anxious about this because of its high salt content and the fact it had often been rolled across the floor. I talked to him about it, and he was quite positive in his response: 'I like it', he said, then taking a grimy handful, he offered it to me 'Want some?'

Children, therefore, do not always do what we expect with the equipment we provide. When we opened our nursery for the Inner London Education Authority in 1978, we were not at first very well equipped. We had inherited a large wheeled crate of blocks and an equally large one of plastic bricks, like Lego, but ten times the size. The children tended to avoid the wooden blocks (our favourite) but loved the plastic ones, though their initial actions were always the same: build a wall as high as you can then knock it down. We tried very hard to move them on to proper brick-laying and so on, but this was not what they wanted nor needed to do. Thirty years on, I can now appreciate that this was their choice and that it fulfilled some perhaps emotional need for excitement and control that was missing in many of their young lives, even if it emptied the local chemist's shelves of aspirin as we tried to cope with the noise. Reflection on these examples over the years has taught me a lesson. We need to think beyond the obvious purpose of toys and equipment to see what each piece means for children and then plan to augment this alternative purpose with other items of stuff. This extract from Paul's book also illustrates this point, not only for parents but also for practitioners who may find themselves under pressure to improve achievement:

> Yet many of today's toys ask children to execute tasks, turning play into performance. David Elkind, a child psychologist at Tufts University near Boston who has studied the effects of parental pressure on children, says that making children believe they need to perform to gain a parent's acceptance dampens natural curiosity. Many toys on the market today may as well have a sticker on them that says imagination not included.
>
> (Paul 2008)

Outside

Next door's cat much prefers to play in our garden (termed 'wild' positively by my husband, but not by the neighbours). This is because there are trees and trellises to climb, bushes to hide in, plants to eat and other visitors, birds, foxes, squirrels and mice, which she can worry and chase though she has negligible impact as a hunter. Our garden is interesting, compared with the pristine decked and lawned area next door. She has a few tumbles, and the squirrels get the better of her from time to time, but she recovers, reconsiders her strategy and tries again. She spends all day, every day, in our garden, only returning home for food and when the weather is ghastly. This mirrors my experience as a child along with many others of my generation and would be the preferred choice, I am sure, of many young children today.

In the UK, there is no legislation in any of the guidance and regulation that early years provision has to have an outside play space. The EYFS Practice Guidance (DfES 2007b: 7) insists, 'All early years providers must have access to an outdoor play area which can benefit the children. If a setting does not have direct access to an outdoor play area then they must make arrangements for daily opportunities for outdoor play in an appropriate nearby location.'

The Statutory Guidance, however, sidesteps this by inserting 'wherever possible' into its requirements (DfES 2007a: 35). As is often the case in UK educational legislation, the section also includes 'should' instead of 'must'.

In any case, insisting that each provider has suitable outside space is currently impossible. Not all state providers, let alone the private and voluntary sectors, have dedicated outside space suitable for young children. Tovey (2007) points out that:

> At the time of writing there are no national standards for outdoor space for early years provision in the UK in contrast to many other European countries. It is therefore possible for nurseries to operate with little or even no outdoor space. It is somewhat ironic that some local authorities have regulations requiring parking space for cars but not play space for children with the result that cars can take precedence over children in the battle for scarce resources.
>
> (Tovey 2007: 8)

In the end, it is how the practitioner uses the outside area which is crucial. The practitioner must be committed to it and see possibilities. There are mixed feelings about 'outside' among the early years sorority, despite the large number of exciting projects offered to us. Bee, who runs the local after school club, went to visit a nursery. It had a good, if small, outside area but it was covered in autumn leaves (it was summer). Conscious of health and safety issues, she asked why these had not been swept up. The manager replied, 'Oh, it doesn't matter. We haven't used the outside all year'. Large, boring outside areas are less interesting than small intimate gardens with plenty to discover and use. This summer, while writing this book, I have been sitting with my laptop, looking out into my garden. It has been good to watch the variety of birds there, from the largest wood pigeon to glimpses of the wren. Occasionally the robin has come to the bird table, and the green parrots that live wild in our area have flocked to next door's tree. This experience is, however, limited: double glazing prevents me from hearing the birds; I cannot feel the heat, rain or breeze; and none of the scents and textures of the garden are available to me. I know as an adult what I am missing. What about the child who never has a chance to experience any of this? In the early part of the twentieth century, Margaret McMillan described how a garden should be for a toddler. This is an extract from her work in designing nursery schools:

> How wonderful the life of the meadow, and the birds that pick at the hearts of the young green things. The rabbits, the tank, the great clouds to which we are sometimes asked to lift our eyes, the vault

of light, the shadows on the white walls. The rustling trees with their great branches, the stones that we gather and carry to nurse in wet pinafores. The pools after the rain into which we diligently go...

(McMillan 1930: 18)

When I was an advisory teacher in a county not far from London, I once visited a school where a need had been identified in the nursery. The children had a nice, big, outside area, but it was boring. Although there was lots of grass, it was flat and had no features to encourage imagination and to challenge the children physically. Plans were drawn up to construct a playhouse in the garden as a first step to remedying this. It would have been easy to bring in builders or to purchase a commercial wooden building, but the head teacher decided to build it himself – with the help of the children in the school. They all got to have a go at digging out foundations, bricklaying and carpentry and something rather special was created. Not all of us may have the knowledge or confidence to do this, but there may be parents, grandparents or others in the community who would welcome the opportunity to do something similar. In another school, a grandfather, whose career had been spent as a carpenter, was asked to construct items for a newly developed early years unit. He built a double-sided easel and then added a complete set of kitchen units to the home corner. In the end, the unit was running out of physical space to house all the items he made.

Questions

- As a child, what were your favourite toys and activities? What did you learn to do through playing with them? Observe a group of children of different ages and see if you can work out what are their favourites. Talk to them about their choices. Is there any way you can add to or extend their interests?

- Many of you will have very little finance to spend on expensive equipment. How do you decide what is essential and how do you prioritise what you will purchase?

- What is your view on equipping your setting with technological toys? Set up a small research project to assess the impact of introducing a new electronic toy into your setting.

- Do you have easy access to an outside play area? How important is this to you? Do you consider that your outside offers 'quality' experiences? Define what you and your colleagues comprehend as 'quality' in this aspect of early years provision. Do you need to revisit what you provide in the light of advice in the EYFS?

References

Athey, C. (2007) *Extending Thought in Young Children,* 2nd edn, London: Paul Chapman Publishing.

DfES (2007a) *Statutory Framework for the Early Years Foundation Stage,* London: DfES.

DfES (2007b) *Practice Guidance for the Early Years Foundation Stage,* London: DfES.

Free Play Network/Playlink (2006) *Places of Woe: Places of Possibility.* Online exhibition at http://www.freeplaynetwork.org.uk/playlink/exhibition/woepossibility (accessed 16 May 2008).

Goldschmied, E. and Jackson, S. (2003) *People under Three: Young Children in Day Care,* 2nd edn, London: Routledge.

Gura, P. (2001) *Resources for Early Learning: Children, Adults and Stuff,* London: Paul Chapman Publishing.

McMillan, M. (1930) *The Nursery School,* London: J. M. Dent & Sons.

Newson, J. and Newson, E. (1979) *Toys and Playthings,* Harmondsworth: Penguin.

Paul, P. (2008) *Parenting Inc.,* New York: Times Books.

Tovey, H. (2007) *Playing Outside: Spaces and Places, Risk and Challenge,* Maidenhead: Open University Press.

9 | Equipment and materials in practice

 The EYFS principles

Using equipment and materials is about the ways in which children use a range of small and large equipment.

- Allow sufficient space indoors and outdoors, to set up relevant activities for energetic play.

- Provide equipment and resources that are sufficient, challenging and interesting and that can be used in a variety of ways, or to support specific skills.

- Use additional adult help, as necessary, to support individuals and to encourage increased independence in physical activities.

The EYFS offers developmental points for each age phase. Scenarios provide ideas in context and additional activities are suggested below. Resources to support the practitioner or the family are included at the end of this chapter. The information here should be cross-referenced to the practical guidance offered by the EYFS documentation.

This takes concentration and skill (4 years 5 months)

From birth–11 months

Development matters

- Watch and explore hands and feet.

- Reach out for, touch and begin to hold objects.

Key words

hand–eye coordination, control, exploring

From 8–20 months

Development matters

- Imitate and improvise actions they have observed, such as clapping, waving.

- Become absorbed in putting objects in and out of containers.

- Enjoy the sensory experience of making marks in damp sand, paste or paint. This is particularly important for babies who have visual impairment.

Key words

imitation, repetition, sensory experience

Scenario 7

Anna watches carefully to see how well Beni is reaching for toys and other objects and is ready to offer him more as he progresses. He likes to explore his hands and feet so Anna uses her stock of brightly coloured mittens and socks to encourage this. Beni sometimes looks puzzled but coos when he reaches them, especially as he sometimes manages to pull them off! Anna also notices how good he has become at kicking. She fills a tin with wooden beads, puts it in a cotton bag and holds it near his feet. He is excited when he kicks it and tries hard to do it again. It's a special game they play together, and Anna changes the container and its contents to provide more interest. Shari is now really interested in malleable materials. She started with playing with her food on her highchair table but has moved on to paint, sand and dough. Anna likes to cook with her, letting her play with the remains if she is making bread, biscuits or cake. Sometimes they put dark chocolate on the cakes and sprinkle it with little silver balls. Shari loves to help in creating this special treat. She likes helping to clean up after this, splashing and swirling the bubbles in the washing up water.

Look, listen and note

Anna is sensitive to the small steps in his progress Beni is making and thinks out things to do to develop his bodily awareness and control. She understands the enjoyment Shari gains from working with soft materials and ensures that there is time each day, often when Beni is sleeping, to share these activities with Shari and show her other things to do. In playing together with her, Anna is able to chat with Shari and introduce her to new words. Does your setting provide:

- items that encourage babies to explore their bodies, manipulate and mouth objects? (Mittens on which simple faces are drawn or socks that make a noise provoke reactions);

- a variety of malleable materials for kneading, prodding, rolling and so on? Do these have different consistencies, smells and colours?

Effective practice

Anna is very aware of the developmental patterns of babies and tod-dlers. She knows the points to look out for and how to encourage development and learning in such young children. She has a range of activities at her fingertips and is creative in providing more when she sees a need. Anna enjoys visiting her childminder network to exchange ideas and is also using her new computer to discover other sources of help and information. Does your setting offer:

- times for toddlers to join in with preparing soft foods and beginning to use utensils, like spoons and shape cutters?

- opportunities for toddlers to play with water, by helping wash up or bathing toys, like dolls and small animals?

Do you let them see what happens if your wash something made from plastic, compared with something made from cloth?

Planning and resourcing

Anna carefully watches the two babies so that she can provide for and encourage the next step in their progress. She notes significant points and photographs what they are each doing. She keeps copies for her records to share with parents but also creates books to share with Beni later and Shari now. Shari loves this, though she does not yet recognise that the baby in the book is her. Anna likes to see what the toy library at the local children's centre has to offer and has borrowed items from there which are too expensive for her to buy. In your setting, make sure that:

- everyone is comfortable with working with very young babies and knows what to look out for, ensuring that a variety of safe objects is available as well as time to play individually or in very small groups;

- toys and equipment offered to or made for you by adults conform to current safety standards (see below) – a folder with ideas can be created which includes guidance and legal requirements, to give to families wishing to provide items.

Home links

Anna shares what happens during the day with the babies' families. Sometimes she gets stuck for a new idea and asks parents for suggestions or if there are particular toys that they enjoy using with their children at home. Sometimes Anna and the families swap. One of the grandparents has constructed wheeled wooden toys for her which Shari particularly enjoys and a butterfly whose wings move, a favourite for Beni. In your setting, ensure that you:

- offer information for parents who have very young babies about development in the first few weeks, what to look for and suggested activities;

- offer sessions which encourage baby play, making sure they are at times when someone from the family can attend;

- display good ideas or suggestions for new equipment for all to see; ask for reviews of how they were used in practice and include photos (if the parents are happy for you to do so).

Additional activities

- As babies begin to grasp things for a few seconds, provide cloth dolls which are easy to hold or rattles that make a sound. Soft rings which have bells or other noises inside are good for grasping and can be placed around babies' wrists or ankles for them to jiggle, to begin to understand cause and effect.

- As babies become able, provide a variety of simple stacking and posting activities. Start with two or three components and gradually increase the number and difficulty. Judge when they are ready to move on, helping them at first then gradually withdrawing your support.

- Find toys for toddlers which offer a reward after an action, for example, toy tills where putting in a coin releases a drawer. A Jack-in-the-Box is another good example of this.

- Encourage toddlers to paint, selecting sponges, crumpled cloths or brushes that are easy for them to handle. Use large sheets of paper fixed to the floor with masking tape so that they can move across. Old pieces of sheeting which can be washed are also useful.

- Have sessions with finger rhymes and clapping games. See if toddlers can anticipate which song it is when the music starts to play.

From 16–26 months

Development matters

- Use tools and materials for particular purposes.

- Begin to make, and manipulate, objects and tools.

- Put together a sequence of actions.

Key words

manipulate, sequence actions, building

From 22–36 months

Development matters

- Balance blocks to make simple structures.

- Show increasing skill in holding and using hammers, books, beaters and mark-making tools.

Key words

control, mark-making, dexterity

Scenario 8

The nursery unit at Edgetown Primary School offers full-time places to 3- to 5-year-olds and holds weekly sessions for mums and toddlers in the year before the children enter the nursery. A new team has worked hard to offer a much more play-based environment for both the toddlers and those already in the nursery. Now, the sessions with parents are relaxed and reciprocal; often a parent will share an incident at home with the group or talk about an outing or a new game. While the adults talk, the toddlers have a chance to use the nursery's equipment. Everything is set out on the floor (and the adults usually sit on cushions, too), and each session offers a different theme – for example, construction and posting, painting and dough. There is always a snack followed by a chance to go outside where digging, painting on a large scale and building with large bricks are on offer. Patti, one of the practitioners, notes that Zara loves to play imaginatively now in the home corner. She is just over two years; she will occasionally play with another child, but mostly they play in parallel, though she will let an adult into her game. She likes to play with real objects but will substitute if she has to. Bricks become vegetables and stacking beakers pans and dishes when she runs out. Her best trick is to 'borrow' her mum's car keys to lock the front door of her 'home' – then lose them! Toby, who is a few months older, loves to build towers and structures. His favourites are bridges, which he likes to place in a large bowl of water with a toy boat. He is beginning to adjust his structures to fit the size of his boats. He becomes quite cross when Zara removes the bricks, but his mum intervenes to offer other materials so that he can practise making different sorts of bridges. Patti observes this, and, next time he comes, she has collected an assortment of plastic pipes, sawn lengthwise, for him to use as tunnels.

Look, listen and note

The practitioners notice that Zara has moved on to play more symbolically, substituting one item for another. They notice how she can carry a pan she has filled with bricks without losing any and can unscrew the tops from containers in the home corner. Toby's coordination is developing well, and he can judge sizes. He sometimes becomes frustrated if he cannot get a new bridge to balance and will then accept some help. Ensure in your setting that:

- you are always ready to offer help to a 2-year-old who has tried and tried but is about to lose interest because an activity has become too hard;

- make sure you can provide alternatives to hold and develop children's interest; talk through what is happening, even if children are not ready to respond fully in speech – they will understand and absorb what you are saying for later.

Snack time is an opportunity for toddlers to eat together, to try new foods and to use new equipment. They will like to watch what others are doing and will want to copy. Some will decide to use a beaker without a feeder lid or to use a fork instead of a spoon.

Effective practice

This team works well with the children who are soon going to attend the nursery and their parents. Sometimes a grandparent or a father will come to the sessions, but this is rare, and the team is considering how to improve this – perhaps by offering themed sessions or a guest speaker which may appeal more to men. The practitioners model good practice to the parents but without being patronising; they are patient with children while they try to do up buttons or put on their socks and shoes, not intervening until the child asks. Ensure that your setting:

- recognises that it is alright for toddlers to eat foods in the best way for them; ensure parents and practitioners do not overreact to mess, especially when 'visiting' the nursery, explaining that the more mess toddlers make now, the more proficient they will become in the near future;

- understands and explains how much practice toddlers need with everyday activities such as dealing with their clothing as the brain and body need to coordinate to make these complex movements smooth and automatic, demonstrating that the best time for practice is not when everyone is in a hurry but when there is time and space and everyone is relaxed.

Planning and resourcing

The setting has a good supply of equipment that belongs to the toddlers' group but will borrow from the nursery, Key Stage 1 or toy library to support special interests or needs. They have 'themed' the toys and equipment into boxes they rotate through the sessions. This not only provides a talking point with the parents but also ensures that items are added every time a need is perceived. The boxes contain storybooks and sources of information; they can be easily taken outside too. Make sure your setting:

- encourages even small children to help to tidy up using real equipment – brushes and dustpans, small brooms and feather dusters are all exciting for small children.

- talks about looking after small animals and pets, encouraging children to bring in photos and items their pets like.

The RSPCA discourages settings from keeping pets, but parents and others may be prepared to bring a pet to visit – one teacher I know brought a sheep and his owner into the nursery and arranged for the sheep to be sheared there, then for the wool to be spun in front of the children.

 Home links

Working together enables practitioners and parents to establish trust and a rapport. They see each other as important, complementary partners in the children's development, and this remains as the children move into school. The nursery offers space to meet, but the relationship flows over into other activities that involve the wider family as well as nursery staff. At Christmas, they all attend a family workshop where decorations are made for all the major festivals. These involve children, families and staff in creating decorations, gifts and cards to celebrate the season. In your setting, do you:

- welcome everyone in the community to events that can enhance their children's learning? Although Christmas offers a lovely opportunity for the children to use their fine motor abilities to create decorations and so on, there are other occasions where parents could offer suggestions from their own cultural backgrounds, for example, Divali (Hindu), Hanukkah (Jewish) or Wesak (Buddhist);

- listen to parents, share ideas and put these into practice?

Additional activities

- Think of activities which include a sequence of movements to build up motor strings (see p. 55). Washing hands or dressing can ⟳ offer practice here – making sure socks are the right way out, putting them on before shoes, then putting them on the right feet and attempting to do them up – with help from a friendly adult.

- Offer toddlers and young children opportunities to work with different sorts of materials. Sand trays can be used with wood shavings, dry leaves, pinecones or plain popcorn. Water trays can have bubbles, food colouring or ice cubes added to them.

- Provide a variety of cutters, rollers and moulds to use with malleable materials. These do not have to be expensive but can be found in bargain kitchenware shops.

- Provide lots of dressing-up items with different fastenings – Velcro, zips, buttons of various sizes. Dolls' clothes can be used too.

- Offer opportunities for children to make meaningful marks. Suggest organising a party, preparing the food, then writing out menus and invitations. These don't have to be perfect or even in words. Squiggles and pictures are fine at this age.

From 30–50 months

Development matters

- Engage in activities requiring hand–eye coordination.
- Use one-handed tools and equipment.
- Show increasing control over clothing and fastenings.
- Show increasing control in using equipment for climbing, scrambling, sliding and swinging.
- Demonstrates increasing self-control in the use of mark-making implements, blocks, construction sets and small-world activities.
- Understand that equipment and tools have to be used safely.

From 40–60+ months

Development matters

- Explore malleable materials by patting, stroking, poking, squeezing, pinching and twisting them.

- Use increasing control over an object, such as a ball, by touching, pushing, patting, throwing, catching or kicking it.

- Manipulate materials to achieve a planned effect.

- Use simple tools to effect changes to the materials.

- Show understanding of how to transport and store equipment safely.

- Practise some appropriate safety measures without direct supervision.

Key words

create, explain, think out, responsibility

Scenario 9

Midshire Primary School focuses on its playground to improve the children's behaviour, both at break times and later in school. The playground is a frightening place to be for the small children who enter the reception class after the freedom and safety of the separate nursery unit. With the help of local early years advisers, the school begins a project with the children and community to take learning activities from the classroom out into the outside. The children suggest things that they would like to see outside to give more opportunities for climbing, jumping and sliding but want areas where those not engaged in the fearsome football games can play with small equipment like balls, hoops and skipping ropes. The school admits children with physical difficulties and it is important that they have easy access to the playground and equal opportunities to play with equipment. To document their suggestions and further ideas for activities, the children are encouraged to record and display their ideas in a variety of ways. They take photographs, for example, in the area and use these to construct 3D models. A variety of materials is introduced, such as clay and papier-mâché, and these are combined with construction and small-world items to create the new playgrounds. Older children help those in the EYFS phase to use the tools and materials safely. The children's ideas are fully incorporated into the revamped outside areas, and all their work is displayed at the celebration that marks the opening of the new outside area.

 ## Look, listen and note

This enabled children to use materials in a variety of different ways which increased their ability to manipulate and manage new tools and techniques. Practitioners noted how the children collaborated to solve problems and increased their vocabulary and ways of explaining what they wanted and needed to do to others. The children were able to refine their use of tools, learning, for example, how to use fine felt-tips and small brushes. Scissor skills improved and practitioners noted that hand preference consolidated in those who were not yet sure which hand they preferred to use. In your setting, ensure that you:

- encourage, but do not force, the use of one hand over the other;

- look for which hand children use when reaching naturally and offer them objects to this hand;

- watch too, what foot a child uses first to kick a ball or climb stairs;

- let them use kaleidoscopes and telescopes to practise looking with the preferred eye; this helps them coordinate their bodies;

- allow children to mix articles from different sorts of play materials when they are creating new worlds;

- ask them to help you sort out and clean the items at the natural end of their play.

Effective practice

This project inspired the children to present ideas in a real context. They recognised that there would be a real outcome to their work, and this gave a sense of purpose and responsibility, particularly when older children were invited to help the little ones. This also freed staff to support young children in learning new techniques, such as using scissors, cameras and computer programmes, as well as reinforcing safety aspects. In your setting ensure that you:

● work together with the children to develop safety rules that all can understand and so respect;

● ask open questions and find ways to reinforce these through stories (make up some of your own) and display agreed rules pictorially near the relevant site;

● encourage the children to improve what they are doing by reviewing whether they have selected the best technique for what they wanted to achieve – a balance is needed here between allowing children to discover the best method through experimentation and passing on adult knowledge and experience; if you do not know, or get it wrong, ask them to help by asking at home or searching books.

Planning and resourcing

A project like this needs enthusiasm and energy not only from the children but from adults too. It has to be effectively led by someone who knows how to work with the community and how to ensure sources of funding, for example, can be found. This school managed this with the help of local-authority support and small grants and gifts from local businesses. The momentum needs to be maintained, especially after the first goal is obtained. Here the staff developed a five-year plan to take the project forward. Everyday resources were found from the school's supplies; extras were purchased, given or requested.

- Audit what you have for a practical project so that you can fill the gaps and think about additional resources.

  - Do you have sufficient items like screwdrivers, tongs or whisks for children who want to play together?

  - Do you have suitable equipment for left-handers or those who have difficulty manipulating tools – not just scissors but also pencil-sharpeners, fat pencils, tape measures or rulers which are numbered from right to left? Left-handers can also have difficulties in unscrewing the lids on containers: make sure you have some which are push on.

- Display equipment and small items where they can be accessed throughout the day. Encourage children to take responsibility for sorting them out after use. This not only helps you but is a good basic mathematical skill.

Home links

The school involved the community fully in this project. Families were invited to put forward their suggestions as well as what they could offer. Staff and parents worked together to remove and rebuild walls, to create mounds in the grass and to returf and to plant a garden. A lot of skills were discovered and honed as the project progressed. Parents also donated small gifts, as well as their time, and were fully involved in fund-raising and planning the next phase.

In your setting, ensure you:

- explain fully what you are hoping to do and ask for help and advice: parents and other family members may have skills to offer that the team does not possess, such as carpentry or needlecraft;

- always ask parents about incidence of left-handedness or poor motor control;

- if a parent is left-handed, ask about his or her childhood and what support was available: what do they do at home and what would they like to happen in the setting?

- share information that you have gathered with them and ask if they have favourite sources.

Additional activities

- Create writing areas where there are a large variety of drawing and writing implements for children at all stages of development. If a child has difficulties with ordinary sized pencils or pens, improvise. Try to prevent the formation of a 'fist-grip' by using a pencil pushed through the centre of a small plastic ball with holes (these are available in pet shops) or a lump of malleable material which will mould to the hand, as well as commercial pencil grips. Keep a range of these. A carpenter's pencil with a rectangular profile and soft lead often helps too.

- Painting with different parts of the body interests children too. Try elbows and feet as well as hands, fingers and thumbs.

- Offer children different ways of fixing things together as well as sticky tape, glue and paste. Masking tape, electrical tape, staplers of all sizes, paper clips, split pins and safety pins can be used – there are good opportunities here to discuss safety issues.

- Have a range of musical instruments that children can use at all times. An area outside which incorporates a 'stage', wind chimes and hanging instruments is a good starting point. Have music sessions to introduce new techniques but also encourage children to create their own. What happens if you put a bell in a buggy wheel or fix a plastic strip to a trike's wheel?

- Making patchwork quilts is a good way to introduce children to a variety of materials and techniques, not all of which need to be based on sewing. Quilts can be used to celebrate a special event as well as a way to document a small child's life events. It can involve the community and practitioners as well as the children.

Must build this bridge (2 years 3 months)

References

There are many books and other resources that reflect the use of different materials and techniques which are interesting for both children and adults. Board and material books for babies can reflect their favourite manipulative toys and can be made with photographs of their own. Here are some of my favourites:

Ayres, P. and Percy, G. (1990) *When Dad Cuts Down the Chestnut Tree*, London: Walker Books.

Bang, M. (1985) *The Paper Crane*, London: Julia MacRae Books.

Andersen, Hans Christian (2004) *The Emperor's New Clothes*, updated by J. A. Rowe, New York: Penguin.

Waddell, M. and Milne, T. (2003) *The Toymaker*, London: Walker.

To provide ideas and instructions to enrich activities in the setting, try these publications:

Frankish, L. (2005) *The Little Book of Clay and Malleable Material*, Husbands Bosworth: Featherstone Education Ltd.

Garner, L. (2004) *The Little Book of Dough*, Husbands Bosworth: Featherstone Education Ltd.

Goodman, S. and Massey, E. (2007) *The Little Book of Fun on a Shoestring*, Husbands Bosworth: Featherstone Education Ltd.

Scott-Walker, M. (2004) *The Toymaker: Paper Toys That You Can Make Yourself*, Costa Mesa, Calif.: Scott-Walker Designs. (This is accompanied by a wonderful website with free downloadable resources: www.thetoymaker.com.)

Wolf, G., Khanna, S., and Ravishankar, A. (1999) *Toys and Tales with Everyday Materials*, Ahmedabad: Tara Publishing. (This one of a series; the others cover child art, puppets and masks and performances.)

If you are fortunate and have someone who can make toys for you, there are many titles which give guidance. Do, however, make sure items meet the safety requirements in The Toy (Safety) Regulations 1995. These can be found at http://www.opsi.gov.uk.

Some of the nicest offer instructions to make wooden toys which will last for a long time:

Makowicki, J. (1996) *Making Heirloom Toys*, Newton, Conn.: The Taunton Press.

Neufeld, L. (2003) *Making Toys That Teach*, Newton, Conn.: The Taunton Press.

Traditional stories and rhymes can be used as source material for this aspect of the EYFS; *Peter Hammers with One Hammer* or *Pinocchio* and *The Elves and the Shoemaker* are good starting points. The ballets *Coppélia* and *The Nutcracker* contain stories about toymakers, and the music can be used as a stimulus. *The Nutcracker* is a Christmas story about a toymaker's gifts, though there is a visit to a land made from sweets, and you need to use your judgement here. (A discussion point?) *Baboushka* offers another interesting story. An animated version of this (with subtitles in Russian) can be found on the CBeebies' website at http://www.bbc.co.uk/cbeebies/stories.

You will be familiar with construction toys such as Brio, Lego, Duplo, K'nex, and Meccano for example. Care needs to be taken when using this equipment in mixed age settings as there are small pieces which may be harmful to babies and small children. You need to consider carefully how you use magnetic toys with young children, such as Geomag and Magnetix. These are good fun but new guidance has been issued which relates to safety issues: The Magnetic Toys (Safety) Regulations 2008. Manufacturers are always adding new support materials and now provide websites that augment their products, offering games to play, stories and sometimes videos. There are sometimes free downloads. Duplo produces *Bob the Builder* materials, which are always popular and relevant here. The Lego pre-school site is particularly interesting. It can be found at http://www.preschool.lego.com. Dorling Kindersley's *Ultimate Lego Book* is a good resource for older children who love Lego.

Making patchwork with children is an exciting way to introduce them to using different materials, tools and techniques. Introductory stories such as David McKee's *Elmer* can introduce them to the idea, then specific stories can be used. Here are some of my favourites:

- Bolton, J. (1995) *Mrs Noah's Patchwork Quilt,* London: Tango Books.

- Bolton, J. (1999) *My Grandmother's Patchwork Quilt,* New York: Doubleday.

- Flourney, V. and Pinckney, J. (1995) *The Patchwork Quilt,* London: Puffin.

- Jonas, A. (1991) *The Quilt,* London: Walker Books.

The website http://www.piecefulquilting.co.uk provides a longer list.

It is estimated that about a third of the population is left-handed. It is important to recognise how to support children in a very right-handed world. These may help you:

- Milsom, L. (2008) *Your Left-handed Child: Making Things Easy for Left-Handers in a Right-Handed World,* London: Hamlyn.

- Paul, D. (1998) *The Left-Hander's Handbook,* 2nd edn, Stourbridge: The Robinswood Press.

- http://www.anythingleft-handed.co.uk

- http://www.left-handed.com.

Appendix 1

Learning to move: moving to learn

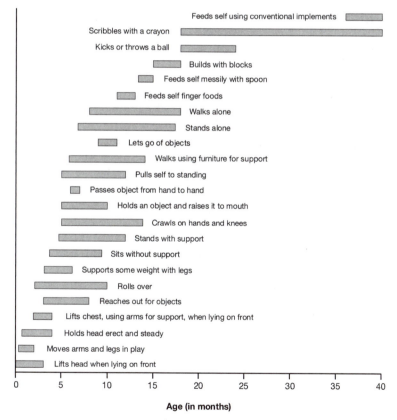

Sources: Adolph (2008), NHS (2007) and World Health Organisation
Multicentre Growth Reference Group (2006)

Appendix 2

Basic cooked play dough recipe

Ingredients

1 cup (110 grams) plain flour

1 cup (300 millilitres) water

Half cup (50 grams) salt

3 teaspoons (10 grams) cream of tartar

2 tablespoons (30 millilitres) oil

Additional ingredients
(check with parents for children's tolerance)

- edible food colouring;
- edible liquid flavourings, such as vanilla or peppermint;
- edible dried flavourings, such as cinnamon or nutmeg;

Method

- If using a dried flavouring, add to the flour.
- If using a liquid colouring or flavouring, add to the water.
- Mix all the ingredients together in a saucepan and heat gently.
- Stir all the time, using a wooden spoon. The lumps will then disappear!
- When the dough firms and comes away from the side of the pan, remove it and place it somewhere safe to cool.

This recipe will keep in the refrigerator for a while, but it is recommended that a fresh batch is made as required. With care, this is a good way to introduce children to cooking and the nature of change in materials.

Further reading

Adolph, K.E. (2008) 'Motor and Physical Development: Locomotion' in M. M. Haith and J. B. Benson (eds), *Encyclopedia of Infant and Early Childhood Development*, San Diego, CA: Academic Press, pp. 359–373.

Bilton, H. (2002) *Outdoor Play in the Early Years*, 2nd edn, London: David Fulton.

Bilton, H. (2006) *Playing Outside*, London: Routledge.

Davies, M. (2003) *Movement and Dance in Early Childhood*, London: PCP.

Doherty, J. and Bailey, R. (2003) *Supporting Physical Development and Physical Education in the Early Years*, Buckingham: Open University Press.

Gavin, M. L., Dowshen, S. A. and Izenberg, N. (2004) *Fit Kids: a Practical Guide to Raising Healthy and Active Children from Birth to Teens*, London: Dorling Kindersley.

Hannaford, C. (2005) *Smart Moves: Why Learning Is Not All in Your Head*, 2nd edn, Arlington, Va.: Greta Ocean Publishers.

MacNaughton, G. and Hughes, P. (2008) *Doing Action Research in Early Childhood Studies*, 2nd edn, Maidenhead: Open University Press.

Moyles, J. (ed.) (2007) *Early Years Foundations: Meeting the Challenge*, Maidenhead: Open University Press.

NHS (2007) *Birth to Five*, London: Central Office for Information (COI) for the Department of Health.

Organisation for Economic Co-operation and Development/Centre for Educational Research and Innovation (2007) *Understanding the Brain: The Birth of a Learning Science*, Paris: OECD Publishing.

O'Leary, Z. (2004) *The Essential Guide to Doing Research,* London: Sage.

Ouvry, M. (2003) *Exercising Muscles and Minds,* London: National Children's Bureau.

Rochat, P. (2001) *The Infant's World*, Cambridge, Mass. and London: Harvard University Press.

Sprenger, M. (2008) *The Developing Brain: Birth to Age Eight,* Thousand Oaks, Calif.: Corwen Press.

White, J. (2008) *Playing and Learning Outdoors,* Abingdon: Routledge.

Wilcock, L. (2007) *The Early Years Foundation Stage in Practice,* London: Step Forward Publishing.

World Health Organisation Multicentre Growth Reference Study Group (2006) *WHO Motor Development Study: Windows of Achievement for Six Gross Motor Development Milestones*, Acta Paediatrica Supplement 450: 86–95.

Useful websites

Centre for Longitudinal Studies, www.cls.ioe.ac.uk

Children's Society, www.childrenssociety.org.uk

Children's Workforce Development Council (CWDC), www.cwdcouncil.org.uk

Dorset Cereals (undated) Edible Playgrounds Project, www.edibleplaygrounds.co.uk

Down' Syndrome Association, www.downs-syndrome.org.uk

End Child Poverty, www.endchildpoverty.org.uk

Every Disabled Child Matters, www.edcm.org.uk

Forest School Shropshire, www.shropshire.gov.uk/forestschools

Free Play Network, www.freeplaynetwork.org.uk

Growing up in Scotland (GUS), www.growingupinscotland.org.uk

Health and Safety Executive, www.hse.gov.uk

Jabadao, National Centre for Movement, Learning and Health, www.jabadao.org

Playlink, www.playlink.org

Sure Start, www.surestart.gov.uk/research